GIFTED PEOPLE

Michael Harper

VINE
BOOKS

Servant Publications
Ann Arbor, Michigan

Copyright © 1990 Michael Harper
All rights reserved.

First American edition published in 1990 by Servant Publications
P.O. Box 8617
Ann Arbor, Michigan 48107

Vine Books is an imprint of Servant Publications especially designed to
serve Evangelical Christians.

Printed in the United States of America

90 91 92 93 94 10 9 8 7 6 5 4 3 2 1

ISBN 0-89283-666-0

The biblical references are from the New International Version, unless
otherwise stated.

Library of Congress Cataloging-in-Publication Data

Harper, Michael, 1931-
  [Those wonderful gifts]
  gifted people / Michael Harper.— 1st Amercan ed.
    p.   cm.
  Originally published under title: Those wonderful gifts,
  ISBN 0-89283-666-0
  1. Gifts, Spiritual. I. Title.
BT767.3.H37 1990
234'13—dc20   89-48576
                                   CIP

CONTENTS

INTRODUCTION

When my wife and I had a deep experience of the Holy Spirit in the Sixties, we were challenged at every step by theological questions. I believe Charismatics, as many of us have become known, gave a good account of themselves. The key issue was the baptism in the Spirit. In this book I have not done what I did in *Power for the Body of Christ,* where I gave a closely reasoned argument for believing what I do. That is not the purpose of this book. The evidence of the realities which we have believed in, concerning the Holy Spirit and His gifts, is now widespread. The Renewal has influenced the whole Church scene throughout the world. But because there is less need now to give a theological explanation for everything, it does not mean that no such theology exists. On the contrary, I believe that Pentecostals and Charismatics have a well reasoned theological understanding of what they have experienced in the Lord, and need to deepen it more and more.

I have mentioned in this book some of our old friends. Since my wife and I had our personal Pentecost in 1962, a new generation has been born. That is why I have included details of some of the people who were household names a generation ago, but may not be known today. They helped to lay a good foundation, so that we who followed them could do the same for the new generation. Therefore, if you do not know the people I refer to, turn to page 123, where I have written briefly something about them.

I hope you will enjoy and benefit from this book. It is written for beginners and for old hands; there is always more to learn about the work of the Holy Spirit. We shall never exhaust the treasures He has to give, nor be bored with our experience of them. They are fresh to all who believe, and the amazing variation of the Spirit's acts still surprises those of us who have been used to them for a long time.

Michael Harper
June 1989

1

THE TIDE SURGES IN

Three hundred and thirty-two million people can't all be wrong! These are the figures recently made available by David Barrett of the largest movement within the worldwide Christian Church.[1]

It all began at the turn of the century. Those involved became known as "Pentecostals" because of their claims to receiving an "Acts 2:4" experience. Acts 2 describes how the early Christians were filled with the Holy Spirit and spoke in tongues. Many before 1900 had claimed to have been filled with the Holy Spirit. But speaking in tongues was largely a novel feature. The critics dubbed it "the Tongues Movement".

If "tongues" was all there was to it, the movement would not have survived a decade, let alone a century. It was missionary from day one, and a "haven of the masses" as one writer has called it.[2] They went out to the poor and marginalised, the ones whom the Churches largely ignored. Today they number 176 million according to David Barrett's figures.

In the Sixties this growing army of Pentecostal Christians were joined by a new movement in the very Churches which had rejected the first wave. It has become known as the Charismatic Renewal. Some have referred to it as "the third force". Lesslie Newbigin wrote in the Fifties of a third member of the "household of God" (as he also entitled his book). Alongside the Catholic and the Protestant strands of Christendom was now a third, the Pentecostal.

In the "swinging Sixties" moral standards reached an all-time low in the West. At the same time some theologians were trying to be "honest to God" and declaring that He was "dead". In the midst of this the Charismatic Renewal came to birth, and now numbers over 123 million throughout the world.

More recently a third wave has moved in. The evangelical world has throughout the twentieth century tried to keep the Pentecostals at bay. They opposed the Charismatic Renewal in the Sixties and Seventies, although their attitude has softened in recent years. Now there is a growing movement amongst Evangelicals with the same experiences of signs and wonders. David Barrett estimates them at 28 million.

David Barrett writes, "all three waves are still continuing to surge in." The growth rate is about 19 million a year or over 54,000 a day. Fastest growth is in the Third World. East Asia is rapidly becoming totally charismatic. Korea and mainland China are the fastest growth points. Probably about eighty per cent of the Christians in China are charismatic.

Other facts to consider:

*** A majority of the world's largest Churches are Pentecostal/Charismatic.

*** They have the highest penetration of the media. They have seized the global initiative in all areas, particularly radio and television.

*** They have the highest number of citywide missions; over 800 a year throughout the world.

*** They are the most generous Christians. Their giving is well above the average.

*** They are the most persecuted, harassed and martyred group in the Christian Church.

*** Contrary to popular belief, they are generally the poorest Christians in the world. Eighty-seven per cent live in poverty. Seventy-one per cent also are non-white and sixty-six per cent comes from the Third World. This is in conflict with the view that they are largely middle class, white and rich.

***They are found in the entire spectrum of Christianity. They speak 7,000 languages and cover ninety-five per cent of the world's total population.

David Barrett sums up his figures, "with this group of Christians now active in eighty per cent of the world's 3,300 large metropolises, all in the process of actively implementing networking and co-operation with Great Commission Christians of all confessions, a new era in world mission would appear to have got under way."

The reason why

This is no flash in the pan, and it is not fading away either. It is the recovery in this century of a basic facet of true Christianity. It needs to be fitted in with other pieces, but the Christian message is poorer without it.

My wife and I have been involved in this incoming tide for over twenty-five years. Our friend and literary agent Edward England has for many years been asking me to write a book on the gifts of the Spirit. In 1987 I wrote a series of articles on this subject for the *Church of England Newspaper*. I am grateful to them for allowing those articles to form the basis of this book.

I hope that this book will help all who read it to see the greatness of God's provision for us. These gifts are still neglected, and even denied by the majority of Christians. It is humbling that people like us are entrusted with such gifts.

Wonderful though they are, they must never be treated as

ornaments to be admired from a distance. They are tools, at times rough and ready, to help build the Kingdom and make Jesus known to all. I am not ashamed to be practical about them. People do want to know, for example, how to prophesy, how to perform miracles and how to heal the sick. The fact that God provides the power as well as the tools themselves, must not disguise the fact that we also have a part to play. We need to have the necessary know-how. That is why this book has been written.

2

THE KINDNESS OF GOD

Giving is the soul of living. Life is the first gift we receive and the last we give away. The magic of Christmas forms in the child's mind the clear truth "giving is good". In the East, where fewer people celebrate Christmas, gifts form an important part of relating to people. So it was natural for the Wise Men when they came from the East to give gifts to the young Christ child. It was their way of honouring Him. To live is to give.

God is the giver of all life. So the giving of gifts is a natural part of what He does. And as God has created us in His image, giving is also a part of what it is to be human. The giving and receiving of gifts form part of the social life of all mankind. My wife and I have travelled to many countries of the world, and our home is evidence of this. Several of the pictures on the walls and ornaments on the shelves were given to us. Some are Chinese, others Korean and Japanese. There are figurines of elephants from Africa, candle-holders from Finland, paintings from New Zealand. Each is a token of love. They are the desire of people to give something of themselves to honour another person.

God has put it into our hearts to do this, because He does it constantly Himself. Being part of His family means we are often receiving thoughtful gifts from His hands. Yet unlike some of us, He is not only generous to His own, He is kind to non-family members, even to His enemies. Jesus described this love for enemies in striking terms. "He causes his sun to rise on the evil and the good, and sends rain on the righteous and the unrighteous' '' (Matthew 5:45). Indeed Jesus defined "perfection" in these terms. There is no great credit in loving your friends, for even pagans do that.

The true God is very different from primitive ideas of deity, which are badly distorted. Primitive people, before God's love has reached them, often think of Him as an all-demanding tyrant, who constantly expects gifts and attention. How far that is from the revelation of God brought by the Lord Jesus Christ!

In addition to this the idea of "giving" demands a complementary "receiving". Jesus Christ was someone who not only gave generously, but received humbly. He was a poor man who depended constantly on the kindness of friends and disciples. He accepted freely the love of Mary who anointed His feet with costly perfume, and wiped them with her hair (John 12:1–8). We are told "the house was filled with the fragrance of the perfume". This was as much the grace of Jesus in receiving as the love of Mary in giving. This is in stark contrast to Peter's attitude shortly afterwards when he refused Jesus' offer to wash his feet (John 13:8).

It is a strange paradox that often those most keen to give find it hardest to receive. Sometimes it can be pride, sometimes lack of self-respect or false humility. We say to ourselves, "I don't need it" or, "I don't deserve it" when a gift is offered. Sometimes our giving is to find favour with people, or placate them in some way or other. But God's giving is pure, for there are no strings attached. He expects nothing in return and gives solely because He loves. Yet His gifts need to be received. This means that those to whom gifts are given need to respond with acceptance and gratitude. It is all too easy to throw God's gifts back in His face and say, "I don't need THAT, thank you very much!"

In John 3:16 Jesus said to a proud leader, " 'God so loved the world that he gave his one and only Son' ''. There was nothing more valuable that God could give. He gave part of Himself. He took the risk of painful rejection, and when that happened He forgave freely. The gift was thrown back at the

Father by some. Others said "yes" to the gift, and were changed by it. John tells us, "He came to that which was his own, but his own did not receive him. Yet to all who received him . . . He gave the right to become children of God" (John 1:11-12).

There comes a day in our lives when we also have to say "yes" to the gift of God. We need to smother our pride, smugness and independent spirit. At that moment we begin to understand the meaning of gifts. There is a fresh discovery that the world is full of God's gifts. We are grateful for every droplet of water, every ray of sunshine, every flower, and see them as tokens of a Father's love for his creation. Before each meal we give thanks. Nothing now is assumed.

We learn also to appreciate the different characteristics people have. The humour of the Finns, the broad smile of the Africans, the politeness of the Japanese, the hospitality of the Americans, all remind us of a God who gives. Everything that is truly beautiful in this life is free, for God makes no charge and collects no taxes. His gifts have cost Him everything. He offers them to us free. We can take them, reject them, or abuse and dehumanise them, and then unjustly cheat our fellow men. But God never does that.

Every year *Time* magazine honours one person, as the man or woman of the year. For 1988 they departed from custom and had instead the "planet of the year". They gave the prize to "endangered earth". Most of the issue was devoted to an alarming account of ecology issues. The earth has been given by God to human kind; it is his great gift. He told us to "fill the earth and subdue it" (Genesis 1:28). He did not tell us to abuse it.

In the Bible we see frequent references to the gifts of God. His creation is a whole network of gifts. He also called into existence a family of faith. Abraham had to learn to trust God from the very moment he stepped out of the security of Ur, the city in which he had lived and grown prosperous. He had to learn to trust in the promises of God, particularly the seemingly impossible gift of a son. And we all have to learn

that the gifts of God are the gifts of a King, who is wise, rich
and powerful.

Amongst much else, Jesus Christ came to reveal in person
a generous God. His life is a profusion of giving. Gifts play
an important part in what He did and who He was. Materially
He had little to give. But what He did have, He gave freely.
The charismatic gifts were a natural part of His life. If we
want to be like Him, they should also be a normal part of ours.

With Jesus there was no "grinding of gears" when He
healed, prophesied, or gave words of knowledge. He didn't
have someone to blow a trumpet every time He did a miracle.
He did everything so naturally. David du Plessis once said
at a conference that we should be "supernaturally natural and
naturally supernatural". That's how it was with the Son of
God during His life on earth.

Jesus opens the way

We are familiar with the sight of a celebrity invited to open
a new road, building or factory. A large crowd gathers,
speeches are made, and the famous person declares it open,
usually cutting some tape or unveiling a plaque.

There are similarities with Jesus' baptism, and we need to
look closely at it. Here was the human commissioning, and
the divine anointing for the years that lay ahead. But it was
also the opening of a new way, the way of the Kingdom.

The details of the story are familiar to us. John the Baptist
declared who Jesus was – the Son of God. Also what He had
come to do. He was to be the Lamb of God to take away the
sins of the world, and the Baptiser in the Holy Spirit, to give
God's power to us to do His will. At first John refused to
baptise Jesus. But Jesus insisted saying, " 'Let it be so now;
it is proper for us to do this to fulfil all righteousness' "
(Matthew 3:15).

Most of the focus has been on the water baptism itself. As
a result the significance of *where* the baptism took place has

been hidden from sight. Some have assumed it was at this spot in the river because the water was deep. Those who believe in water baptism by immersion have pointed this out. But there were other places where water was deep.

All this has obscured the real reason why John chose this spot, and why Jesus went there to be baptised. *It was at the point where the Israelites entered the Promised Land.* Through His life and death Jesus was going to open the door into another and far more important Promised Land. He was opening the way to the Kingdom, whose arrival He was about to announce. Later the gifts of the Holy Spirit were to be part of the divine dowry made available to the Bride of Christ at Pentecost. Just as the Israelites entered the Promised Land by faith, so we enter the Kingdom of God with all its challenges, dangers and opportunities.

Later in this book we will look at each of the gifts in turn. We will give examples from the life of Jesus of how He used the gifts to serve people. These will encourage us to do the same. Most of the gifts are also to be seen in the Old Testament. We shall give some examples. Also we will share some modern occasions when the gifts have been experienced.

The gifts of the Spirit must never be isolated from the personal value of those who have them. These gifts can become a menace when they are depersonalised. It used to be said that we should seek "the Giver not the gifts". That is only half true. A better statement is, "the Giver *and* the gifts".

Before we can go any further we need to think clearly about who we are. Jesus prepared His disciples for the time when He would be taken away from them. The bonus they were to receive was the active presence and power of the Holy Spirit. Like their Master they were to be "kings in the Kingdom". They, and their successors, were to be born again by that Spirit, to receive kingly blood, to be members of the royal family of Heaven. They were then expected to behave like kings; to follow the way their Master took. To do the things that He did, and be like the person He was. We are their true successors. We too are "royals".

3

THE ROYALS

The royal family in Britain is a remarkable phenomenon. They are the subject of endless comment, and the focus of constant attention. Wherever they go they are followed, and whatever they do and say is recorded. Interest in the "royals" is by no means confined to Britain. They are often front page news in the world's media.

They are a constant reminder of what royalty means. And we need this. For Christians also are "royals". We are "King's kids". We are children of the King of kings.

It is important for us to realise that one aspect of true kingship is the giving and receiving of gifts. Being in God's royal family means we are of all people the most blessed. In Ephesians 4:8 Paul quotes Psalm 68:18, which is one of the great royal Psalms. " 'When he ascended on high, he led captives in his train and gave gifts to men.' " It is interesting that Paul changes the direction of the giving. In the Old Testament version of this text it reads, "you received gifts from men". Jesus Christ changed that. Instead of royalty being a name for greed, in which kings ravished their subjects and taxed them out of existence, it now becomes a word for generosity. The heart of royalty is now giving rather than receiving.

Paul applies the words of this Psalm to what happened after the Ascension of Christ. He gave gifts. In particular He gave power to people to serve in His name. Jesus Christ at Pentecost equipped the Church with the gifts of the Holy

Spirit. Many of them had been evident before in the Old Testament. But now they would be given to all the royal family of God; they would enable that family also to be generous donors. They would be "gifted" in order to be givers.

Before we look at the Pentecostal experience, we need to consider those to whom this promise was made. There is no status in the Kingdom of God and the Church of Jesus Christ. We all come in at the same level. By contrast there was privilege in the Old Testament. There the royals were set apart, and the priests served in the temple in an exclusive fashion. Kings and priests had very different roles. Woe betide anyone who stepped out of line! When King Uzziah went into the temple and started behaving like a priest, he was struck down with leprosy (2 Chronicles 26:16-21). The same was true of the prophets. They were chosen and anointed by God not men, and they were scarce on the ground.

How things have changed since Jesus Christ! According to John we are a "kingdom and priests to serve his God and Father" (Revelation 1:6). The family of God is to be priestly. That is to say *all* are able to enter God's presence through the sacrifice of Jesus Christ and able to offer acceptable worship to Him. All are also to be "prophetable". That means that *all* are able to hear and speak the word of God. It is also to be kingly; *all* of us are members of Heaven's royal family. We have been given authority to extend God's Kingdom throughout the world. We are joint heirs with Christ of that Kingdom. It is mind-blowing!

The primary reason why we are baptized in the Spirit is because we are God's royal family and He wants us to reign with Him. The main reason why the gifts of the Spirit are freely given to us by the Lord is to exercise God's authority and power in a practical way. That is why it is so important to know about the Kingdom of God.

The Kingdom that God wants to extend on this earth is very different from earthly kingdoms. The way we exercise power differs from the way it is done by the world. Although

God's Kingdom is not of this world, it is very much in it, and has a practical effect on it. The Kingdom is not just a nice idea or theory. It is not complicated theology. It is God's rule on earth as well as in Heaven: it is signs and wonders; it is repentance and faith; it is the way God changes people and then the world. Some have wrongly interpreted the Kingdom in political terms. By doing so they have distorted it.

Jesus quite clearly said "no" to a political solution to the world's ills. Even after He had risen from the dead His friends asked Him " 'are you at this time going to restore the kingdom to Israel?' " (Acts 1:6). They were still thinking in terms of political liberation. Jesus answered this question by saying that they would receive power when the Holy Spirit came on them. Pentecost "restored" the Kingdom. It was the real Kingdom, and every act of God before then pointed to it. Once the door of the Kingdom was opened by the Lord, the gifts of the Holy Spirit were given to the Church in abundance. *When the Church today moves obediently in kingly power, the gifts will be there for all to see and hear, and the Kingdom will have come.*

Sadly, the opposite is also true. It is God's will for us to live like "royals". We are sons and daughters of God. Yet often we live as if we were menial slaves or second class citizens. We have royal rights and royal responsibilities. Paul says that there are two ways of serving the Lord, as sons or as slaves. He tells us there is a spirit of fear and slavery, and the Spirit of sonship (Romans 8:15). Elsewhere he says that we are no longer under the law (like slaves), but we are "sons of God through faith in Christ Jesus". He goes on later to say, "you are no longer a slave, but a son" (Galatians 3:26, 4:7).

The Church is full of struggling Christians. They strain to please their Lord. They work harder and harder to satisfy their Master. From the pulpits heavier and heavier burdens are placed on them. They feel condemned not justified. They have little joy in their service. They are not a good advertisement for the Kingdom of God.

It is easy to see why such people seldom receive the gifts of the Holy Spirit. They feel unworthy. They are more conscious of their sins than the smile of God upon them. Their hard toiling for the Kingdom closes them to the generous gifts God wants to give them.

We need to be constantly reminded who we are. Here the Holy Spirit helps us. He is called the Spirit of adoption or sonship (Romans 8:15). He enables us to exclaim, " '*Abba, Father*' ". The more we allow the Spirit to control our thinking and our attitudes, the more we will live as sons rather than slaves.

This is important for another reason. We don't just live in a vacuum. We face daily spiritual warfare. Satan wants to push us around. Satan sowed lies into the mind of Jesus when he said to Him, " 'If you are the Son of God. . .' " (Matthew 4:6). He will do the same with us; he will want to deflect us from our royal progress, doubt our status as the King's sons and daughters, and keep us in the misery of slavery. Jesus came to liberate us from that, so that we might live in dignity not shame.

We see a good example of this in the story in Genesis of Jacob and Esau. Our sympathies often extend to Esau, for Jacob was crafty and deceitful. But Jacob with all his faults had one fine quality. He saw the importance of the birthright. Esau didn't, and was prepared to exchange it for a bowl of lentil soup. That was the difference between these two men.

Our attitude to our birthright is crucial. It will determine all we do for Jesus Christ, and the extent to which we will be effective in the Kingdom of God. To live the way we should, we must know who we are. We must value our birthright above all else, and not sell it, as Esau did, for temporary satisfaction.

In the next chapter we will be considering the power of the Holy Spirit. Power is not some impersonal force, as displayed, for example, in the film *Star Wars*. It is vitally linked with the person of the Holy Spirit, and has to do with Jesus being Lord. It is not given so that we can lord it over people. To get the right view of this we need to know what it is to be in the royal family of God. When this happens, there will be no danger of power overwhelming us, or of our trying to use it for the wrong reasons.

4

ROYAL POWER

In 1987 Jeanne and I celebrated our twenty-fifth anniversary of what Jesus called "the baptism in the Holy Spirit". Our view of what happened and how the Word of God explains it have not changed through all these years. When we started out we were regarded as freaks and largely ignored. But what joy it is to see the situation completely changed now. It is no longer an unusual experience of God's grace; today it is shared by so many. What is the essence of this blessing of the Lord's?

Doctrine or experience?

The main use of the term "baptism in the Holy Spirit" in the New Testament relates to what happened at the first Pentecost. Jesus promised the disciples that " 'in a few days you will be baptised with the Holy Spirit' " (Acts 1:5). We find the same use of words by Peter in Acts 11:16, when he tells the Church in Jerusalem about the Caesarea incident recorded in Acts 10. This is usually referred to as "the Gentile Pentecost".

The baptism in the Holy Spirit is a doctrine because it is part of the ministry of Christ and is promised to all Christian believers. Jesus is described by John as "he who will baptise with the Holy Spirit" in the same breath as "the Lamb of God" and the "Son of God" (John 1:29 – 34). Just as Jesus' death on the cross, and His rising from the dead are doctrines, so also is the ministry of Jesus as the Baptiser. He came to save us and to baptise us in the Spirit. We see this also in Hebrews 6:2 when the writer refers to "instructions about baptisms" as a doctrine on a par with "the resurrection of the dead" and "eternal judgment".

On the other hand the baptism in the Holy Spirit is also an experience. All doctrine is of this nature. For instance the Cross is intended to be an experience as well as a doctrine. Paul writes about being "crucified with Christ" (Galatians 2:20). The same is true of the Resurrection. Christians according to the same writer have been "raised with Christ" (Colossians 3:1). The day of Pentecost was an experience springing from the teaching of Jesus Christ, and fulfilling what the Old Testament taught and promised. Scripture gives us confidence to search out doctrinal truth and the fruit that comes from it, though not to seek for experiences for their own sake. The promises of God are not merely to be admired as "truth". They are to be entered into by faith, so that they become experiences which deeply affect our lives.

Baptism or fullness?

Some have argued that we should not use the term "baptism in the Spirit", but call it "the fullness of the Spirit". It is true that the experience recorded in Acts 2 was described as "fullness". But let's remember that Jesus, as we have seen, promised a "baptism". So which is it?

The answer is "both", and we may use both terms. If we have to distinguish between the two, "baptism" refers to the doctrine because it is Jesus who does the baptising, not the Church; "fullness" refers to the experience, telling us what happens.

There is still a stigma attached to the term "baptism in the Spirit". There may be historical or personal reasons for this, which need to be taken into account. But in the final analysis it is the way Jesus described it, and we should not be ashamed to use it ourselves.

There is an important value in the term "baptism in the Holy Spirit". It is arresting, descriptive, and "different". It shocks us into doing something about it. It challenges us to compare our lives with those of the early Christians.

One or many?

There is an old adage, "one baptism, many fillings". These are sound words. It is not possible when we read the New Testament to see baptism as something that is repeated, except when we read of the "baptism of suffering". Water baptism is a once-only event, and should never be repeated, because it is a rite of initiation. So is Spirit baptism. The early Christians were to receive more fillings, notably the one we are told about in Acts 4:31. But they were only baptised in the Spirit once. It is important to keep this distinction. But baptism is always "with a view to", that is to say a door into a new level of Christian experience. How far we progress depends on how much we trust and obey.

We may well need to be re-filled at different stages of life. But we can only be baptised in the Spirit once.

Life or power?

It is vital for us to see the difference that exists in scripture between water baptism and Spirit baptism. The event at Pentecost in Jerusalem was not a once-off booster rocket to get the Church into orbit. It was given to other groups and individuals also. In Acts 8:12–17 the Samaritans were not only baptised in water, but they had hands laid upon them, which resulted in the Holy Spirit coming upon them. In Acts 10:44–48 the Holy Spirit came on Cornelius and his friends who were later baptised in water. In Acts 19:1–7 water baptism was followed by the Holy Spirit "coming upon" the converts in Ephesus. In all these cases water baptism and Spirit baptism are separate and distinct. They happened at different times, and are the expression of two different doctrines – regeneration and the empowering by the Spirit.

I believe we can see this distinction as two operations of the one Holy Spirit. In the first, the Holy Spirit comes to give new life and the new birth. Water baptism is the outward and visible sign of that new birth. While in the other the Spirit anoints or empowers Christians for their witness and ministry. Jesus said, " 'you will receive power when the Holy Spirit comes on you, and you will be my witnesses' " (Acts 1:8). He did not promise them life because they already had it through the Holy Spirit.

Guarantee or assurance?

The baptism in the Spirit guarantees nothing – it depends entirely on how faithfully and obediently we follow the Lord afterwards. Both Ananias and Sapphira were baptised in the Spirit because this was normal in the Church in those days. Yet shortly after they had received it they experienced the judgment of God because they had lied to Him. In this respect water and Spirit baptism are alike. Simon Magus in Acts 8:13 was baptised in water, yet had a very carnal view of the work of the Spirit. Peter had to say to him, "your heart is not right before God . . . you are full of bitterness and captive to sin" (v. 20–23). The same, alas, can be said of some who are baptised in the Spirit today. Some fall into the same sin as Simon in wanting power for the wrong reasons. *When praying for people I have always found resistance to the Holy Spirit when that person is wanting power for the wrong reasons.*

Yet it is important to see that one of the side benefits of being baptised in the Spirit is a deeper assurance of our sonship. This is partly due to the fact that it is Jesus who baptises us in the Holy Spirit and through it enables us to "do the works that He did". Thus we are assured of the fact of our sonship. We begin to behave like it, and share more fully in the ministry of Christ. Paul touches on this when he writes in Romans 8:16, "the Spirit himself testifies with our spirit that we are God's children."

It is baptism in the Spirit which has initiated millions of Christians into the life of renewal. It is important that we understand what has happened, as well as why we have been so blessed. Power is not primarily given to bless us. Rather it is so that through us others may meet with Jesus Christ and make Him Lord of all. It is sad to meet some Christians who are still basking in a blessing received years ago, and not moving forward in the Spirit. Our spiritual health should not be measured by a past experience however deep, but by the present condition of our walk with the Lord.

Receiving this experience

I am going to be practical. Why not? After all God made the world in a practical way, and I have yet to meet a farmer who isn't practical about how to get the best out of his land. I find it difficult to imagine God promising us something so wonderful, and then leaving us in the dark as to how to obtain it.

Of course our intentions need to be sound. But Peter in the Acts knew how to handle that old scoundrel Simon Magus when he tried to jump on the bandwagon for the wrong reasons. Since we need the power to enable us to do the will of God, we may assume there is a way of receiving it which is simple to understand.

Not everyone will get there by the same route. I have found that the Holy Spirit treats us with respect. He is a "gentleman" as David du Plessis used to say. He won't force us to do anything which is unnatural or embarassing. But equally He will not kowtow to pride or selfishness. We have to submit to Him, not He to us.

We must not shirk the fact that this is an "experience". Something happens to us. We have all grown up in the atmosphere of rationalism. We have received an endless stream of this thinking at school, through the media, and alas, in some of our churches also. So we are not open to things happening which cannot be explained. We find it difficult to accept that God does give us something more than good ideas or advice: that He actually *does* something in us. The way to receive all God's gifts and promises is through prayer, faith and commitment. But first let's look at possible channels through which we may receive this experience.

The channels

We have made it clear that there is only one "baptiser", and He is the Lord Jesus Christ. He may or He may not choose to use people to bring us into this blessing. But He is the donor. We receive it only from Him. When we look at the Acts we do see people involved in a ministry of the Holy Spirit in this specific sense. In fact Paul in his letter to the Galatians refers to the one "who supplies the Spirit to you" (Galatians 3:5 RSV). It is perhaps hard for us to think of a person, even an apostle, as a supplier of the Spirit!

But it is no accident in the Acts that God chooses a narrow-minded Jew called Peter to bring Pentecost to the Gentiles (Acts 10), and John (with Peter), one of the disciples who asked the Lord to fire blitz the Samaritans, to minister the Spirit to new Samaritan believers (Acts 8). I have known of occasions when through human pride people have told the Lord who they wanted to have minister to them, and the Lord has sent the most unlikely person. I met some years ago a strict and narrow-minded Baptist, who was very critical of Anglicans and the ministry of women. So the Lord chose a female Anglican to be the instrument of His blessing! The Lord has a way of doing things that may seem strange at the time, but afterwards can be seen as wise and positive. What better way to bridge the Jewish/Gentile/Samaritan racial barriers than for Gentiles and Samaritans to receive through strictly kosher channels!

There are a few basic principles which we need to observe about this experience. This is in addition to the one already mentioned – that the Lord is the Baptiser. Water baptism needs to be protected from an individualistic approach; as if it is all about ME making a decision to follow Jesus Christ. Paul says in 1 Corinthians 12:13 that we are baptised "into one body". The unity and the proper ordering of the Body of Christ is part of what this is all about. So baptism in the Spirit is as much a "body" experience as it is an individual one.

This means that we should submit all this to the Body of Christ, the Church. In fact, some Anglicans do receive this experience at their Confirmation. Others receive on their own. This is usually where there is no climate of faith in the church. There may be no one who knows how to help them, or who believes in the experience and the rightness of seeking it. This was certainly my case. No one laid hands on me, and it came quietly and privately in my own heart. However, thousands do receive at public meetings.

But it is good to have someone to pray for us. It has been helpful to scores of people. In some cases it may be a one-to-one situation, when a person sits beside us and lays their hands on us. In other cases it can be a more public occasion when many are prayed for, and counsellors move amongst them praying for them as they are led by the Holy Spirit. In Acts 19:1 – 7 Paul laid hands on twelve of the Ephesians. The need for the unity of the Church lies behind some of the stories in the Acts. As we have seen, it was most important that the racial division between the Jews and the Samaritans should not be transferred to the Church. Thus the fact that Peter and John came down from Jerusalem to pray for the Samaritans to receive the Holy Spirit, helped to cement that relationship for the future.

Check list for receiving the promise

We need to prepare carefully for this baptism in the Holy Spirit. We should examine ourselves. Mainly we need to direct our attention to Jesus Christ. Do we really want Him to be Lord of all? We may need to repent of known sins; it may be necessary to put things right between ourselves and others. This may include forgiving or asking forgiveness of others.

Heart-searching is important, but don't prolong it beyond reason. The Devil will always show us something else, or get us to believe we are just not good enough. Be honest about everything, and leave it in the hands of God.

There are three factors which are necessary to receive this promise of God:

1. Faith

It is by faith and patience that we receive God's promises (Hebrews 6:12). Faith is the inner conviction that what God has promised to us He will supply. Jesus called the baptism with the Spirit " 'the gift my Father promised' " (Acts 1:4). If we do not believe that God keeps His promises, then we make Him out to be a liar (1 John 5:10). If we find we can't or don't believe, that is not the end of the matter. Confess your unbelief to God, believe in your forgiveness, and then trust what the Lord says. Faith is both a fruit and a gift of the Holy Spirit. So there is a plentiful supply of it in Heaven, and all for the asking!

2. Prayer

Jesus said that God would give the Holy Spirit " 'to those who ask him' " (Luke 11:13). There is a small detail which is often overlooked in the story of Jesus' baptism. We are told that Jesus received the anointing of the Holy Spirit "as he was praying" (Luke 3:21). In the Acts we see the Holy Spirit received through prayer and usually the laying on of hands.

3. Action

The first two I have mentioned are perhaps obvious. They seem to put the ball firmly in God's court. We ask Him to do something. But there is a response we need to make also. The Lord puts the ball back into our court. We need to act upon our request.

I would guess that failure to take this factor seriously is still the major hindrance to people being filled with the Holy Spirit.

Jesus was constantly getting people to do something in response to His initiatives. The lame were asked to walk, those with paralysed arms to stretch them out, the blind to see and the lepers to get their cure registered with the authorities. *In other words to act in line with what has just been asked for.* It's as simple as that.

4. A sign

When the disciples were filled with the Holy Spirit at Pentecost, their faith response or action was to speak in tongues. It was something *they* did. God wasn't going to do it for them. It was human action, yet inspired by the Holy Spirit, for speaking in tongues is a gift of that same Spirit.

Speaking in tongues is something we do; but with the help of the Spirit. We speak, and the Spirit gives us the words to say. It was the sign to Peter, when he was in the house of Cornelius (Acts 10:44–46), that the Gentiles were receiving the Spirit without first becoming Jews. It can be for us also a useful sign or evidence (though not a necessary one) that we have been baptised in the Spirit.

Royal power, once we have received it, leads us into a new dimension of Christian living. The Kingdom of God becomes a new reality to us.

5

FIRST MOVES IN THE KINGDOM

So, once you have been baptised in the Holy Spirit, what comes next? The early stages can sometimes be a disaster area. But most people seem to recover and get through this trial zone, gaining a lot of wisdom on the way. So let's look hard at it, and move ahead with the maximum benefit and the minimum of trouble.

It is, I think, only reasonable to expect a degree of immaturity with those who have been recently blessed. The trouble is that enthusiasts are not the most popular of people, especially when they show up our own lack of zeal. There are always those in the Church, like the elder brother in the parable of the prodigal son (Luke 15:11 – 32), who have been around a long time, yet who have for various reasons missed the best that God has for them. When someone comes "home" like the prodigal son, they resent the fuss that is made of him.

It is worth remembering also the story in Genesis of Joseph's brothers, and their attitude to their charismatic younger brother when he shared his dreams with them. We realise how angry people can get when others are more spiritual than they are. We all know the "holier than thou" accusation that some make against others. It is even worse when it becomes a "more spiritual than thou" affair.

Dealing with relationships

One thing has happened for sure. We have a new and
dynamic kinship with the Lord Jesus Christ. This is the surest
sign that we have been filled with the Holy Spirit. We feel
closer than ever, and our faith has reached a new peak. But
people are another matter, and we cannot avoid facing up
to the challenges here.

Marriage partners

Blessed indeed are those couples who enter into this experience
together. In our case there was only a four-day gap. But some
may have to wait some time before their partners are able
to share in it too. Some unwisely put pressure on their partner
to "conform". They drag them to meetings, or leave suitable
books around, hoping they'll read them. Couples often play
games with one another when one of them receives something
the other one doesn't have. Most of this will be counter-
productive. The targeted spouse will take evasive action and
miss God's best plan for them. It is an unproductive game
to play.

It is important in all our relationships, as we shall see, to
share as soon as possible what has taken place. It would be
hurtful to our marriage partner if they were to find out from
someone else what has happened to us. We need to reassure
them that we love them, and that we are not going to force
anything on them. On the contrary, we want to share it
together, like everything else in our lives. We should explain
simply what has taken place, and assure them that the God
who has blessed one will bless the other also. It has not made
us better than them, or different in any fundamental way.

We need to recognise that everyone is different. This is even
more true in marriage, as we tend to team up with someone
who is not like us. It is good that the Lord treats us all

differently. We should not expect our partner to receive in the same way as we did. We should let it come naturally in God's way, and not expect it to be a carbon copy of our own.

Singles don't have this particular problem. But they may be sharing a flat or house with others, and so the same principles apply. We always need to respect the feelings of others, and not force this on them. Almost certainly their curiosity will be aroused. They will watch us like hawks. We need to have a simple and unselfconscious attitude to them, letting them read our lives like a book, and making sure it is the Lord who is really in control of what we do and say.

Church and minister

The other person we should share it with as soon as possible is our minister. This may be difficult, especially if he is known to be anxious about charismatic experience and activity. But again it is much better for him to hear it from us than from third parties. He is going to find out sooner or later anyway.

When you see him you need to reassure him that you are not going to join an "opposition" party (most churches have at least one!). Also that you respect and recognise him, and will submit to him as far as possible in the church. Certainly you should not start a new group without consulting with him, and you should seek to integrate your experience in the life of the church as far as you can.

There may well be others in your church who are also moving in the power of the Spirit. It will be natural and healthy to meet with them, and receive all the help and encouragement you can from these people. But we need to be careful not to appear to be "ganging up" against the minister and others in the church. We should continue in whatever church work we have been involved in before. We should seek to be loyal, consistent and conscientious.

We should seek to stay in our church, even if there is strong opposition to what the Holy Spirit is doing. However, there may come a time when we should leave and move to a more sympathetic church. Today there are many churches moving in renewal. But this is the easy option we should refrain from using until we have clear guidance from the Lord. Normally this takes time to arrive at, and we should be patient. Let us remember there would be far fewer churches in renewal today if people had left because of opposition. Again and again it has been the loving and faithful witness of lay people that has turned the tide. So be patient, and trust in God who changes people.

But if you are the minister, what should you do? I know of a variety of approaches from the full treatment on the very first Sunday, to keeping silent until found out. The people entrusted to us will find out soon enough; if they don't, one might begin to wonder what one has received. Our preaching, teaching, counselling, praying – and everything else – should be enhanced by such an experience. There is no need to shout it from the pulpit; it should be self-evident, for the Holy Spirit is the true witness.

Discovering one's gifts

All Christians are gifted people. Like everyone else, Christian or not, they have natural gifts which should have developed during life, and which are dedicated to Jesus Christ when we are converted, or at some other time in life. These gifts also need to be empowered and freshly inspired by the Holy Spirit. Sometimes our gifts and talents can be hindered for various reasons. Some people don't develop their full potential. The Holy Spirit helps a great deal in the developing of natural as well as spiritual gifts. He is the Creator Spirit, and so He helps to bring out creative gifts in us, some of which may have been hidden from childhood.

When we come to the charismatic gifts of the Spirit, there is a special role and responsibility that leaders have. Whether ministers or lay, they need to discern the gifts in others. People need to be encouraged to share their gifts with the wider body and not hide them. The man with the one talent was wrong just to preserve it. We are not to treat the gifts as museum pieces, but tools of great practical worth. Gifts should be "traded" or they will be lost or given to others.

Shy people need to be drawn out, and the brash restrained so that they use the gifts in a positive way to edify or build people up. Faith will need to be more strongly established. We cannot assume anything these days; often people have a poor knowledge of the Bible, and so have little in their bank of knowledge. There should be consistent Bible teaching; at the same time there should be a constant expectation that the faith that is built up on this Bible teaching *works* – that is, it leads to the free moving of the Holy Spirit, so that things happen. Without such expectation, the Bible becomes a dull textbook, or merely a history of the past activity of God.

Defeating sin

Everyone I know finds sin more subtle and difficult to combat after being baptised in the Spirit. We experience "highs" which we never knew before, and "highs" are dangerous places to be. Two of Jesus' temptations were in high places, the top of a mountain and the pinnacle of the temple (Matthew 4:5–11).

There is sometimes a narrow line between the spiritual and the sensual. Baptism in the Spirit often releases feelings and emotions, which, if not handled properly, can lead us into moral danger. When our faith and expectation rises, it is easier to throw over restraint and take risks than when it is low. We can more easily launch into adventures which make it harder to resist temptation. For instance, in the area of finance we can be extravagant on the basis that the Lord will provide. We may be attracted to the "Prosperity Gospel", and feel that a Mercedes or BMW is essential to maintain the right image and prove we have "faith". The distinction between what I want, and God's will becomes blurred.

One of the results of Charismatic Renewal has been a new intimacy between the sexes. Twenty years ago men and women shook hands with one another, unless they were married. Now they hug and kiss. Some of this is healthy; Christians were inhibited, and often coldly distant from each other. But there are obvious dangers also, which need to be recognised and acted on.

There can also be extra tensions in our marriage. This is especially true when only one partner is baptised in the Spirit. It can be a further factor in the gradual drifting apart which may lead ultimately to separation and divorce. When one partner becomes frustrated because the other does not share the same spiritual experience, and then finds a person who does, the alarm bells ring loudly.

It is important to realise that we become a special target of the enemy when we get blessed in this way. He is out to get us. We will look in a moment at the new intensity of spiritual warfare we become engaged in. But human weakness, or "flesh" as the Bible calls it, is still our most vulnerable area for the enemy to attack.

Discerning the enemy

It has often been pointed out that Jesus' temptations in the desert came immediately after His anointing with the Holy Spirit. Many a friend of mine has had a similar experience, going quickly from the peak of the mountain to the depth of the valley.

The temptations Jesus had to face were closely linked to the experience He had just had. They were to do with "power", which is the basis of most temptations. Our sexual desires and greed for money are two powerful instincts, which can easily get out of control. They are not only powerful in themselves, they also enable us to have power over others. But power is, in and of itself, a source of temptation. This is particularly true after we have been baptised in the Spirit.

As our faith rises, so do the relevant temptations to use power for the wrong reasons. Power can be as intoxicating as alcohol. It can act like a drug if we are not careful. It can then destroy us and others through its influence.

We are inevitably pitched into spiritual warfare of an intensity we never thought possible. Satan throws everything at us. He tests our experience with lies about ourselves and others. He criticises us through other people, for he has always been " 'the accuser of our brothers' " (Revelation 12:10). He tempts us to be proud of our achievements, and to throw our weight around. Our natural craving for attention becomes another area where the enemy thrives. All this and more were the lot of Jesus Christ, and He was victor over them all. This should encourage us. We too can have the victory through Him. But let the key words be, "watch and pray".

Developing worship

Wherever and whenever the Holy Spirit is present amongst the people of God there will be worship. His work is to glorify Jesus Christ. So it is only natural that when we are filled with the Holy Spirit the result will be praising hearts and praising lips.

We will find in our private prayer life that praise will figure much more often and spontaneously. It will keep bubbling up, and will be hard to restrain. We should let the Spirit be free to fill us with praise, for it plays its part in developing a healthy and balanced life. Most people feed on negatives and it shows in their faces. Positive praise and worship disinfect us of egotism, drive out the negative, and open us up to the guidance and inspiration of the gifts of the Spirit. It is revealing that it was during worship in Antioch that the Church there was led through a prophecy to send out Paul and Barnabas (Acts 13:2).

Worship for the Spirit-filled person becomes a much more physical thing. We will find our body moving with the music, our feet tapping out the rhythm. We will find it natural to lift our hands, and will know that this was a normal response to worship as recorded in the Old and New Testament.

Dealing with the past

We will be tempted in the blinding light of the present to dismiss our entire past. That would be a great mistake. Most of us have some links with the Church and with Christian education, although this influence is less than it was. It does not glorify God if we fail to give Him thanks for all that He has done through our past life.

Sometimes we will call in question our baptism, either because we were baptised as children, or because we were not believers when it took place. I am touching on a sensitive subject, and there are those who would urge such people to be re-baptised, or baptised properly as they would prefer to put it. I would rather preserve the objectivity of baptism as something which we should receive only once. All true experiences which follow it are equally to be accepted with gratitude. God is not limited, but neither is He mocked. We should accept our baptism and not feel we can improve on it. At the same time we should recognise that the faith that activates the blessings promised in that baptism may well come at a later stage. To demand re-baptism can be a subtle departure from the faith principle, for it is after all faith which makes any symbolic act powerful.

Baptism is not the only thing in the past which needs to be recognised. It is popular today to scorn the past, and to criticise and condemn parents, teachers, ministers and our families for not having given us what we needed in the way of Christian teaching. This is not a healthy response. Almost certainly some of the reasons for our present blessing will have come from this past, and it is right to recognise this.

Dynamic witness

I have left the best to last. When Jesus spoke to His disciples about the day of Pentecost, He told them clearly that the power they were about to receive was to make them witnesses (Acts 1:8). We must never forget that this is the main reason why the Spirit has been poured out. We can live a reasonably faithful life without the power of the Spirit. But we are helpless without the power of the Spirit in the task of evangelism. That is the main reason why He is given in this way.

The early Christians were compulsive witnesses. Peter and John boldly told their religious superiors, " 'we cannot help speaking about what we have seen and heard' " (Acts 4:20). When we are filled with the Holy Spirit we too seem compelled to share our faith with others. It comes out more naturally. There is a joy and confidence we did not have before. We are more deeply assured than ever that the Lord has saved us and changed us into different people. We want to tell the whole world about it.

*　　*　　*

So we take our first steps in the new life of the Kingdom. To start with it is wiser to walk than to run. Some running can come later.

6

WISE WORDS

We are now going to look at the gifts of the Holy Spirit, one by one. In the last few years there has been a growing acceptance of these gifts in the Christian Church. But acceptance is not enough. We are to experience them as tools in God's service, and that is more difficult. I plan to be practical. I want people to be excited about the potential of these gifts in their lives and their churches. But chiefly to enjoy sharing in them to the glory of God and the good of people.

In a new book published in the United States, Larry Christenson has referred to "the strategy of the Spirit".[3] He goes on to explain why the gifts of the Spirit are particularly significant *today*. He sees the Spirit coming against entrenched humanism, "a religion that has planted the autonomous human being firmly at the centre of all things." A belief system, however biblical and orthodox, will not break through the shell of humanism. The new and much wider experience of the gifts of the Spirit is a proven weapon of immense power against such forces, because it comes from a radical dependence on God.

It is no accident that the first gift that Paul mentions in 1 Corinthians 12:8 is "the message of wisdom". Wisdom is a quality highly regarded in most societies. A cursory look back at our lives will almost certainly reveal words that came to us suddenly and which have helped us in an important way. Equally, there are other words we wish we'd never said or written, and actions we have later regretted. If only we'd acted more wisely life would probably have been smoother for us,

Gifted People

and less unpleasant for others. We all could do with more wisdom. But we need to notice that Paul is not here writing about general wisdom, but a specific manifestation of it – *words*. The gifts of the Spirit are concrete and specific. Sometimes we may not know which gift it is, for some overlap one another, but we are left in no doubt when a gift is manifested. It makes its mark on the situation.

We need also to distinguish between wisdom and wit or cleverness. Shakespeare quotes the words, "better a witty fool than a foolish wit". In some ways we can see folly as the opposite of wisdom. Wit is a mere embellishment, a way of expressing something which may be wise or foolish. Wisdom is a much deeper quality than cleverness. The response that it incurs is also different. Cleverness can humiliate or set people apart. Wisdom, which owes nothing to education, usually encourages and edifies.

The Old Testament equivalent of the passage in 1 Corinthians about spiritual gifts is surely Isaiah 11:1–3. This is one of the most famous predictions of the coming of the Messiah. Again the first quality mentioned is "the Spirit of wisdom and of understanding". That is what one looks for in a person upon whom the Spirit of the Lord rests. The Lord commended Solomon when he asked for " 'a discerning heart to govern' ". It is said that God gave Solomon "wisdom and very great insight" (1 Kings 3:9, 4:29).

Almost immediately the wisdom of Solomon is put to the test. Two prostitutes came to him each claiming a baby as their own. Solomon suggests cutting the child in two, so revealing who the real mother was. That was a word of wisdom, inspired by the Spirit of God (1 Kings 3:16–28).

We will, of course, expect to see the same gift in the life and ministry of Jesus Christ. The Spirit *rested* on Jesus. In fact the Spirit was given "without measure" with a fullness never before or since matched. The prophecy of Isaiah was fulfilled. The spirit of wisdom was evident in all that Jesus said and did.

We see this in two areas in particular – His healing ministry and His encounters with His enemies. Wisdom was needed because He had voluntarily allowed Himself to be stripped of all but normal human assets. Jesus, according to Paul, "emptied himself", thus exposing His weakness. So He was utterly dependent on the divine assets of the Holy Spirit for His successful and faithful ministry.

When Jesus healed the man with a withered hand in the synagogue on the Sabbath, He was guided by the Holy Spirit in a situation in which a trap had been set for Him (Matthew 12:9–14). His enemies were watching to see Him do some work on the Sabbath, i.e. lay hands on the sick person, which He often did. This time Jesus simply spoke healing words, which was prompted by a word of wisdom. His enemies were thwarted again.

Towards the end of His earthly life Jesus had to go through a barrage of public attacks. The Pharisees were eager to trap Him into saying things that could be used against Him in a future trial. A classic example is the question about whether or not it was right to pay taxes to Caesar (Matthew 22:15–22). Jesus turned the tables on His adversaries by the use of a word of wisdom.

It is interesting that Jesus promised the same gift to His disciples. He knew that they too would be confronted with powerful human authorities bent on using anything to condemn them and discredit their beliefs before the public. But in Luke 21:15 Jesus promised them, " 'I will give you words and wisdom that none of your adversaries will be able to resist or contradict' ". Again in Mark 13:11 Jesus told His disciples, " 'Whenever you are arrested and brought to trial, do not worry beforehand about what to say. Just say whatever is given you at the time, for it is not you speaking, but the Holy Spirit.' " This was not advice for sermon preparation! Jesus was encouraging those caught in the open with no previous knowledge of the questions that would be asked. They would be entirely dependent on the gift of the word of wisdom, and it would be given them.

There are many examples in the Acts of the Apostles of the

way this gift operated in the lives of the early Christians. A famous occasion was when Stephen was confronted by his enemies. We are told in Acts 6:10, "they could not stand up against his wisdom or the Spirit by whom he spoke." It did not save his life, but the gift enabled him to speak bravely and boldly for the Lord. In passing it is interesting to notice that when Stephen was chosen they were looking for men who were "known to be full of the Spirit and wisdom" (Acts 6:3).

We also notice this same gift of the word of wisdom in the writings of Paul, and Peter is swift to acknowledge it (2 Peter 3:15). Again and again he handles delicate issues with remarkable wisdom, not least the controversy with the Corinthians over the practice of spiritual gifts in the Church. We could all usefully emulate the wise way he holds together freedom and responsibility, the Spirit and the Word.

What of today? The same Holy Spirit is with us, making us like the Lord Jesus Christ, "in whom are hidden all the treasures of wisdom and knowledge" (Colossians 2:3). When I was first renewed in the Spirit I was often sharply questioned in public. I still remember the help the Lord gave me.

During the Sixties I was invited to speak at an evangelical conference in the North of England on the gifts of the Holy Spirit. After I had finished speaking, an evangelical vicar, who is now a bishop, got to his feet and contradicted all that I had said, in a harsh and judgmental manner. As he spoke I felt the warmth of the Spirit rising in me. I felt more sorry for him than angry! Having finished his work of demolition, I rose to my feet to answer him. Like John Wesley once said, "the Lord filled my mouth with arguments." My answers, and the gentle spirit with which I was able to give them, convinced one of the clergy present, and he was baptised in the Spirit shortly afterwards.

Another way of looking at this gift is to see it as "divine tact". Jesus was never fanatical. He displayed a sensitive response to His enemies, which we could call "tact". He did not waste words. Christian leadership needs this quality. This is especially true when a church is going through the process of renewal. An example of this was in one of the first Anglican churches in Britain to be renewed. It was St. Mark's, Gillingham, and the vicar then was John Collins. People were upset when the first people were baptised in the Spirit and spoke in tongues. One of the older leaders in the church came to the vicar and complained about what had happened. After expressing his criticisms he added, "and they are a strange lot anyway." To which John Collins replied, "Perhaps they need this more than you do, Bert." The remark defused the situation, and led very quickly to this man being baptised in the Spirit himself and many others too.

One is reminded constantly of the book of Proverbs, which is a rich mine of wisdom. It should be compulsory reading for all involved in renewal. Do you remember the words, "a gentle ["soft" AV] answer turns away wrath, but a harsh word stirs up anger" (Proverbs 15:1)? How often we regret the harsh responses we make; how truly they "stir up anger"! If we can only pause for a moment and send an arrow prayer to Heaven, it makes all the difference. God gives us the wise words to speak. We also can be reassured by the words of James, "If any of you lack wisdom, he should ask God, who gives generously to all without finding fault, and it will be given to him" (James 1:5).

Many times during our travels God has given us this gift when we have had difficulties at frontiers and with immigration officials. But we should all remember the old English proverb, "Wise men change their minds, fools never." The Holy Spirit shows us when we are wrong and when our mind needs to be changed. This is a gift worth coveting and cultivating.

7

LEARNING SECRETS

There is an obvious link between the word of wisdom and the word of knowledge. If God gives you a word of knowledge, you need a word of wisdom to know how to use it! As with all the vocal gifts of the Spirit, the possession of a gift does not necessarily mean it should be used. Lack of wisdom in the use of the gifts has been a major deterrent in their operation. When Joseph was given words of knowledge in the form of dreams about his brothers' bowing down to him, he lacked wisdom and would have been better to have kept quiet instead of telling them what he had seen (Genesis 37:5 – 11).

Not everyone agrees how to interpret Paul's references to the "word of knowledge", and what scriptural examples are apt. Arnold Bittlinger sees nothing particularly "supernatural" in the gifts in general and this one in particular. He defines it as "the old message spoken in the new situation in such a way that it still remains the old message . . . to speak the word of God with its unchanging sharpness into the contemporary situation . . ."[3] He gives the Sermon on the Mount in Matthew 5 – 7 as the supreme example in the New Testament. Personally, I would classify that as "prophetic preaching" and associate it more with the gift of prophecy.

The late Donald Gee, one of England's foremost Pentecostal pioneers, took a similar line to Arnold Bittlinger. In the Twenties and Thirties there was a rash of words of knowledge, particularly from German Pentecostals, which caused embarrassment in Pentecostal circles. Often they were a moral indictment of Pentecostal leaders who were present at the time (e.g. that someone was a secret smoker or consumed alcohol forbidden to Pentecostals). Donald Gee in one of his books spoke critically of this use of the word of knowledge and tended to relate it entirely to the relevant exposition of the Word.

Bittlinger and Gee may well be right. There is, however, plenty of evidence in the Bible that another interpretation is nearer the mark, namely that the gift is what it says it is, hidden knowledge which is revealed by the Holy Spirit. It is "learning secrets", as I have called this chapter. It is particularly relevant in the healing ministry and it has been brought to prominence by John Wimber in recent years.

It has, it must be said, been around much longer, and I first saw it in the Sixties through the ministry of Harry Greenwood. It occurred at the first charismatic conference I organised at Stoke Poges Manor House in 1964. After breakfast on the Sunday, Harry gave us a list of sicknesses in people present which were going to be healed, and later we prayed for them.

In John 14:26 Jesus says of the Holy Spirit that He " 'will teach you all things and will remind you [bring to your remembrance] of everything I have said to you.' " Although this remark should not be limited to the word of knowledge, it gives us an insight into one of the main functions of the Holy Spirit, to be the revealer of truth. We need to look at some examples in the Old and New Testaments to see how the Spirit revealed knowledge sometimes of political and military significance.

One of the classic examples comes in 2 Kings 6. The king of Aram is at war with Israel. Whatever move he made Elisha was able to communicate the details of it to the king of Israel. It reminds one of the cracking of the German "Enigma" code in the Second World War, so that throughout the war we knew of the movements of the German forces throughout Europe. Unlike the Germans, the king of Aram discovered what was happening. His officers told him, " 'Elisha . . . tells the king of Israel the very words you speak in your bedroom.' " The Holy Spirit was for Elisha like a modern bugging device. There are many other examples in the stories of the prophets. Samuel, Elijah and Elisha seemed to have constant knowledge of facts which were only revealed to them by the Holy Spirit. I believe we can rightly call these "words of knowledge".

When we come to the Gospels and the Acts there are abundant examples of this gift being useful to Jesus and later to His disciples. In John 4:4–26, for example, Jesus talks to a stranger while sitting alone by a well. Jesus asks her to go and bring her husband. She says she has no husband. Jesus replies, " 'You are right when you say you have no husband. The fact is, you have had five husbands . . .' " How did Jesus know? And how did Jesus know Zacchaeus' name, and that He was going to stay at his house (Luke 19:5)? How was He able to describe Nathanael so accurately (John 1:47)? How was Jesus able to know exactly how Lazarus' illness was progressing, so that He knew when he had died before the message about it had arrived (John 11:1–14)? But the gift is most clearly manifested in the healing work the Lord did. He seemed to understand each person, and particularly what was hindering them from being healed. When we ask "how", we are bound to answer – "the Holy Spirit".

The early Christians had the same gift, and used it sometimes in tricky situations. Peter, for instance, was able to expose the deceit of Ananias and Sapphira when he challenged them about some of the money that they had kept back for themselves having agreed to share everything (Acts 5). He was to know beforehand about Sapphira's death (v. 9). We see the Holy Spirit directing the strategy of evangelism. Philip receives a word of knowledge about the spiritual hunger of the Ethiopian official, " 'Go to that chariot and stay near it' " (see Acts 8:29). Similarly Ananias is given clear directions to go to Paul, even the name of the street (Acts 9:11). There are many other examples of crucial guidance being given through words like this, and sometimes also in dreams, as in Paul's vision of the man of Macedonia (Acts 16:9).

It is one of the ironies of our day that in an age of unprecedented knowledge, when the prophecy of Daniel, " 'Many will go here and there to increase knowledge' " (Daniel 12:4), seems to be having new fulfilment, we are still so ignorant, particularly about our human nature and the spiritual realities of the Kingdom of God. One of the main developments in the Christian healing movement in recent years has been what is called "inner healing" or "the healing of the memories" as Agnes Sanford called it. It is well established that bad memories, traumas of early childhood, or even in the womb during pregnancy, do cause sickness, both physical and emotional. Quite often these memories are repressed either because they are too painful to recall, or because they have been forgotten altogether or their significance is not realised. We have seen the effectiveness of the "word of knowledge" in releasing these memories so that they can be healed by the Lord. The counsellor in prayer either "sees" them in a vision, or words connected with them are brought to their mind by the Spirit.

I have been present when there have been remarkable words of knowledge in the ministry of people like John Wimber and the late Kathryn Kuhlman. I am convinced of the authenticity of them. Some accuse such people of practising clairvoyance. I think this is unjust. Clairvoyants do possess remarkable skills, although some are charlatans. It does no good to deny this. On the other hand if the enemy uses such powers, why should not God's people do similar things in the power of the Spirit? After all we see Moses beating the magicians of Egypt at their own game. Jesus did the same when He had power encounters with demonised people. So did the disciples in the account of the amazing growth of the Church recorded in the Acts.

To receive a word of knowledge one needs the adoption of two attitudes, expectation (it can be given to me), and faith (it will be given to me). Then one needs an ability to wait on the Lord and to learn how to receive revelation into one's mind, and the courage to test it out. You may be wrong, but that is no crime!

During a conference some years ago I had a picture given me in my imagination. I saw a cellar, and the steps leading down to it. I began to share this with those present, and as I did so the picture became more detailed. The Holy Spirit used this to bring healing to a man present. It was a word of knowledge since it gave him revelation about things that had happened in his life, which had caused him traumas, and as a result sickness. As the picture unfolded he re-lived that part of his life and was healed.

I often find that the Lord gives me words of knowledge when I am praying over people, not neccessarily for healing. Sometimes a word has confirmed a call to new work. At other times a word of rebuke or correction, which came in this way, brought healing at a later date.

We need to recognize the dangers of such power. Paul in 1 Corinthians 13:2-3 says, "if I . . . can fathom all . . . knowledge . . . but have not love, I gain nothing." In 1 Corinthians 8:1 he warns, "Knowledge puffs up [like a balloon!], but love builds up." The greatest safeguard against the abuse of this gift is the fruit of love in our lives.

Let me say again, the word of knowledge is not intellectual know-how stored in our minds and recalled at will. For example, it will not help us if we compete in the television *Jeopardy* competition. God has given us minds in which to store information. But this gift is not about that at all.

It includes the ability given to one person to recall what another has forgotten. You may remember that King Nebuchadnezzar not only asked the magicians, enchanters, sorcerers and astrologers of Babylon to interpret one of his dreams, but also to guess what it had been about because he had forgotten it! Fortunately Daniel was able to do so (Daniel 2).

It is also the power to reveal what is unknown to a person, which cannot be discovered any other way. Since the Christian religion is one based on revelation not human reason, it should not surprise us that such a gift of revelation is available for the people of God.

It is also a way of assessing what is relevant and important in given situations. It helps us to sort out a lot of factors, which present themselves to us in a complicated fashion. For instance, when we try to plan a strategy for evangelism or pastoral care in our church, miraculously God places in our thoughts a way to bring strands together, harmonising people and their gifts and arriving at solutions to complex situations.

It is also a way of exposing lies, errors and half-truths. As we have seen already Peter had this gift when he told Ananias and Sapphira that they were liars (Acts 5:1–11), with dire consequences for them. We need to beware of superstition, which can grow like a cancer wherever people are just religious. The word of knowledge will cut through this sometimes dense undergrowth, and reveal the truth. The Holy Spirit is the Spirit of Truth. When He fills us, we are committed to joining His campaign against all that is false to that truth.

8

PLEASING GOD

Perhaps one of the surprising gifts of the Spirit is the gift of faith. We would not expect to find it numbered amongst the gifts that God gives because we think of it primarily in terms of our response to God. But here it is, and you will also find it in Paul's list of the fruit of the Spirit (Galatians 5:22). It is the only word to be found in both lists. Obviously faith is a key word in the Bible, and we are told that without it one cannot please God (Hebrews 11:6). That is why I have called this chapter "Pleasing God".

Faith certainly gave pleasure to Jesus Christ, and when it was absent it caused Him pain. He wept over the faithless city of Jerusalem, but rejoiced in the Spirit when His disciples returned triumphantly from their encounters with Satan (Luke 10:21). Few gave the Lord more pleasure than the Canaanite woman and the Roman centurion, neither of whom were Jewish. To the former He said, " 'I have not found such great faith even in Israel' " (Luke 7:9); and to the latter, " 'I have not found anyone in Israel with such great faith' " (Matthew 8:10).

But we need to look a little closer at the word itself. Because it is listed amongst the gifts of the Holy Spirit, we can rightly presume it falls into the same category as the others. In other words it is a gift "for others" rather than for oneself, and *this* faith is not necessarily given to every Christian. For obvious reasons we are not here speaking of the faith that brings us salvation, which the Philippian jailer needed when

Paul and Silas told him to " 'Believe in the Lord Jesus, and
you will be saved – you and your household' " (Acts 16:31).
That kind of faith is given by God to everyone who believes.
No, this is the gift of faith which helps *others* to believe.

The name of George Muller will always be closely linked
with "faith". He was a famous apostle of faith in the
nineteenth century, who started a number of orphanages. His
appeals for money were addressed only to the Lord. He never
asked people for it, and did not even make his needs known.

He always said that he did not have the gift of faith himself.
He thought that everyone should have faith like he had,
though not necessarily to live as he did. I believe he was
modest, but mistaken. George Muller had a special gift of
faith, because through it he inspired millions of others to trust
God, though without necessarily choosing his way of life, or
having the same gift.

I have met people who have this gift. To be with them,
and to hear them speak and watch them in action, one can
feel one's own faith temperature rising. They are not boastful
people, always talking about their spiritual conquests and
achievements. They do not exaggerate, nor are they
unbalanced or hyper-spiritual. They just ooze faith! It is so
much part of them they don't need to say anything. It just
comes to those in their company. One of those who influenced
my wife and me many years ago was a Yorkshireman called
Cecil Cousen, who then edited a magazine called *A Voice of
Faith*. Just to look at Cecil was to inspire faith!

At a time when a friend of mine was holding back from
making a bold step forward in his work, he went to hear John
Wimber. He heard John speak of faith as another name for
"risk". As a result my friend boldly went forward, and the
Lord blessed his project.

We must remember that this is a gift of God, like all the
other "spirituals" as Paul calls them. But it is fed and
encouraged by the reading of the Scriptures. In essence it is
something which God gives according to His will alone.

We should not assume that a person with such a gift is good

to have around. Such strong faith can make life uncomfortable for those who live and move within its influence. Remember Caleb and Joshua when they returned to the Israelite camp to report on their recce into Canaan. "Caleb silenced the people before Moses and said, 'We should go up and take possession of the land, for we can certainly do it' " (Numbers 13:30). These were words of faith coming from men who had the gift of faith. But the other spies did not have the gift, " 'they are stronger than we are' " (v. 31), they said. " '. . . the LORD is with us. Do not be afraid of them' ", said the faithful pair (Numbers 14:9). Then we are told that the whole assembly talked about stoning them. Many a Christian has had a God-given vision and has had to face flak from all sides as a result. The story has been repeated many times. But we need to remember that both Caleb (still asking for "mountains"!) and Joshua made it into the Promised Land in the end, whereas the others didn't. So much for their critics. Those of us who have faith to believe God for a tough assignment need to persevere even when we get a barrage of negatives from others.

But why does faith please God so much? There are two simple answers, one of which is obvious but the other easily missed. The fruit of faith is an attitude of heart and mind which acknowledges our dependence on God. It is saying in effect, "I am a child of God and He is my Father, and that is the way I always want it to be." Unbelief is saying that God is a liar (1 John 5:10). In as many words we are declaring that He is untrustworthy. To put it another way, "faith" is a relationship word. When there is faith, there is relationship with God, and He is pleased. This is all so obvious, yet it needs to be restated time and again because we are so often substituting other things in the place of faith. The most common is "work". We are beguiled into thinking that it is our work that pleases God. If we could only work a little harder, He would be even more pleased with us. The fact is that our work does not interest God as much as we think it does. It is *we* who are the object of His love; He cares for us more than the work we do.

But there is another aspect of faith that is less obvious, and indeed often overlooked altogether. *Faith is creating an environment for God to work.* What God does is much more important than what we do. The Lord is free to work when there is faith present. And it is the gift of faith which is so valuable in this context. Obviously Caleb and Joshua were unable to create the environment of faith for the invasion of Canaan. It had to wait until later. But pre-eminently we see this faith environment created by Jesus. He was very sensitive to what we sometimes call "atmosphere" or "vibes". If faith wasn't there, as in Nazareth, "he did not do many miracles" (Matthew 13:58). Only a few got blessed. When it was there, "he healed all their sick" (Matthew 12:15).

There is also another story about Jesus which illustrates this important factor. Bethsaida was notorious for its unbelief. It was one of the towns Jesus picked out for particular criticism because of its lack of faith (Matthew 11:21). When Jesus and His disciples came to this town and wanted to heal a blind man, Jesus had to remove him from this unbelieving environment. So He took him by the hand and led him outside the village (Mark 8:23). He was then healed.

If I have learnt anything in the last twenty years it is sensitivity to the atmosphere of the Holy Spirit. I think I can be almost one hundred per cent certain about this. After a short time in a meeting I know what the faith temperature is. It can change during the meeting and often does, especially as people respond positively to the Word of God as it is taught. It can change the other way also, as people rebel against and reject that Word. Faith, therefore, is preparing the way for the coming of the Lord in power. When faith is present, He comes, and since that is what He longs to do, it pleases Him. Faith is an operational as well as a relational work. There is the *gift* of faith as well as the *fruit* of faith.

Churches should be, amongst other things, a company of people who, when they are gathered together, create through their faith a welcome and open attitude to the Holy Spirit.

How can we do that? Here are a few tips:

1.   Reject negative input. Moaning about life in general destroys faith. Negative attitudes need to be rebuked. Some people feed on judgment and condemnation; they like to harp on it. As they do you can feel the spiritual temperature of the church going down. Prophets of doom always see the worst side of things.

2.   Encourage positive input. Paul says, "whatever is true, whatever is noble, whatever is right, whatever is pure, whatever is lovely, whatever is admirable – if anything is excellent or praiseworthy – think about such things" (Philippians 4:8). He was writing to a Church whose weakness was criticism. It is faith not criticism that pleases God, and our job is to build people up, not knock them down.

3.   Study and *do* the Word of God. Let it be proclaimed in every situation. Let people *see* the works of God as well as hear the Word of God.

God wants us to move mountains as well as molehills. Let's start by all means on the molehills, and graduate to the mountains. But let us not take our time over it. There is much to be done for God. We need to be people who not only have faith in God, but who urge on others to have the same through our sharing the gift of faith with them.

9

THE PLURAL GIFT

Healing is the most talked about and most practised of the gifts of the Spirit today. The reason for this interest is plain. Sickness affects everyone, and in the Western world at any rate health is now seen almost as a human right, even when our life style is anything but conducive to it.

It is interesting to note that divine healing assumes major proportions in the Third World and the United States for different reasons. In the Third World medical care is strictly limited. Doctors and drugs are scarce. In the United States, where the opposite is true, one can't afford to be ill, as medical care is so expensive.

There has been a long debate as to why Paul writes about the *gifts* of healing. Why the plural? The most common answer is that people who have this ministry often have specific areas where they seem to have success, whereas in others they don't. It is as if the Lord appoints and anoints "specialists". Some have, for example, specialised in what has become known as "inner healing". Others practise "signs and wonders". Then there are those who are primarily involved in a deliverance ministry.

Whether this explains why this gift is plural or not, there are a wide variety of ways in which divine healing is practised. All the way from the strong shouting of Reinhard Bonkke, the humour of John Wimber, the steady and consistent ministry of people like the London Healing Mission, the Dorothy Kerin Trust, and Wholeness through Christ; or the

Order of St. Luke, an international work which started in the Episcopal Church in the United States. Then there is the use of healing in evangelism through people like Oral Roberts and Don Double. There is also the vital work of many doctors, nurses, and other members of the caring professions. They often add to their medical skills compassion for their patients and a faith in their recovery. Truly there are many *gifts* of healing.

We hear a great deal about divine healing today. It is no longer the preserve of a few heroic pioneers. It is exciting to see how many churches today have healing near the centre of their life and ministry. It is an important recovery of a biblical ministry, which was central in the Kingdom work of Jesus Himself, and afterwards in the Early Church. In 1 Corinthians 14 Paul discusses problems which arose over some of the gifts, particularly speaking in tongues and prophecy. But we can assume from the lack of any correction or rebuke in the healing work at Corinth that the Christians there had both success and balance in their use of these gifts.

One indication of the importance of the gifts of healing is that most of the other gifts operate with them. For instance the gifts of the word of wisdom and the word of knowledge can serve in the counselling which is usually needed to make a clear diagnosis. The need for such skills widens out in divine healing, because we have to cover the spiritual dimension which is usually ignored by the medical profession.

Faith is so vital, especially, as a gift given by those involved in the healing ministry to the sick person. Some healings will be in the category of miracles, and we shall be referring to that gift in the next chapter.

It is of interest to note that if we list the healings of Jesus we find deliverance ministry, or exorcism as it is sometimes (erroneously) called, the most frequently recorded. So the gift of "distinguishing between spirits" is vital for some kinds of healing to take place. Many of us have also found speaking in tongues a useful tool. It can be used either as a quiet form of prayer and meditation while ministering to sick people, or as a part of authoritative commands to Satan or evil spirits when a deliverance from their power is needed. So we find all of the spiritual gifts in the centre of the healing ministry.

Another reason why this gift is often needed is simply because there is so much illness. Many people become ill, or know people who are. In spite of all the drugs and sophisticated treatment available, sickness is as universal as sin. This provides many chances both for evangelism with signs and wonders, and a sensitive pastoral ministry to the Lord's people. I do not believe it is God's will to heal everyone in this life. Some of my friends in the Charismatic Renewal will disagree with me about that! Nevertheless He is clearly healing many today just as His Son did during His earthly life, and the Early Church did according to the Acts of the Apostles and the later records of the Church in the early centuries.

There is no question about it, *healings increase in direct relationship to the level of faith.* You can plot a graph, more faith, more healing. Less faith, less healing.

Of course there are dangers in the work of healing. One has only to recall the cultic forms of healing which have occurred many times in the history of the Church. They were popular in the Middle Ages when the alleged healing powers of relics and shrines brought fame and financial rewards to many. There have always been examples of those (like Simon Magus) who want to "buy" power for the wrong reasons. But the abuse of a gift is not a good reason for its neglect. On the contrary the more there are false gifts, the more we should expect and welcome the real thing. There is no such thing as a counterfeit unless the real thing exists also! The main ministry of the Holy Spirit is to be the revealer, the One who leads us into all truth. And He is also the actualiser, the One who gives us power to heal the sick in Jesus' name. The Spirit who reveals the truth about healing will also help us to discern the abuses of the gifts, and how to handle each situation when it occurs.

In May 1987 I was suddenly taken ill in Yugoslavia. The

previous evening I had been speaking about the healing work of the Lord and we prayed for many people afterwards. The following morning I had amnesia, and was taken into the intensive care ward of the local hospital with the symptoms of a stroke. I was later reminded of the way Peter was arrested and taken to prison. But his Church did not give up, rather it prayed as it had never prayed before! The Church in Osijek, where we were, did not give up either. Within twelve hours the symptoms went, my memory returned and two days later I walked out of the hospital and flew back to England.

Was this a divine healing or a miracle? We can't prove it was a miracle, although I believe it was. The Lord has planted in our bodies a whole immunity system that defends it, and can set a healing process in motion spontaneously. The body can heal itself. Or is that another way of describing a part of divine healing? In my case drugs were administered, but according to the doctors in the hospital this did not account for the sudden improvement. Whatever the answers are I'm personally thankful that at that crisis in life I was surrounded by people who believed in the gifts of healing.

No one will ever solve all the mysteries of divine healing. Why did Smith Wigglesworth, for example, who was used all over the world to heal the sick, fail to heal his own daughter, who was born stone deaf? And why did the wife of Alexander Boddy, the Anglican Rector who brought Wigglesworth into the baptism in the Holy Spirit, heal many sick people while herself confined to a wheelchair? Why was Dennis Bennett's first wife not healed of cancer? Dennis discusses this in a moving chapter in his book *Nine O'Clock in the Morning*.[4]

We cannot answer these questions in this life. They are a mystery. But we do know that God has not withdrawn the gifts of healing. The Holy Spirit still makes them available to us today, and we can receive them when we trust Him.

Let me try to answer some practical questions.

When should we practise divine healing?

There is no one answer to this question, and we should try to be as flexible as possible. In the Epistle of James we are told that a sick person should "call the elders of the church" (James 5:14). This would suggest prayer in the home, and the initiative is clearly placed on the sick person. This is one line to follow, and we need to instruct people about this, so that they will know what to do when they or others are ill.

Another setting could be in private counselling. If deliverance ministry is in mind there should be at least two people present. If a healing need arises, then it would be natural to respond at once to it, and prayer for healing would form a perfectly normal part of the counselling session.

Healing services have become quite common in our churches, but they can be self-defeating. They tend to be for the more elderly members of the church, and often become a club for the chronically ill. Healing should be done more openly in the church, and should involve the young as well as the old, the healthy as well as the sick.

If we are to practise divine healing in public worship, it is better to include it in the normal services as part of ministry to the whole person, not just the physical part. There should be teaching included, which may not necessarily be about healing. One of the most favourable settings for this ministry is at the Holy Communion service. It is hard to think of a better prayer than one which comes in the *Book of Common Prayer*. These words are spoken when the Bread and Wine are given to people, "preserve thy body and soul unto everlasting life."

We have already seen that unbelief will always be a hindrance to divine healing. We are told that Jesus could do no great work in Nazareth "because of their lack of faith" (Matthew 13:58). The move to set up healing services has at least in part been motivated by this. It is essential to create an atmosphere of faith, and initially this cannot be done in some churches. So we have to do it "on the side", making sure that those who come do have faith.

In the life of Jesus and the Early Church healing formed part of the Gospel message of the Kingdom. Jesus and the early Christians proclaimed a Kingdom message which included "signs and wonders". In recent years this has received new focus through the ministry of John Wimber and the Vineyard Ministry in the United States.

In the light of the increasing commitment of Churches to a Decade of Evangelism in the Nineties, it is important to include this dimension in all aspects of Church evangelism. Just as Jesus healed people who were not His disciples, so we can and should do the same in His name today. And we cannot make their commitment to Christ a condition of their receiving healing. Experience, however, has often shown that many non-Christians do believe when they see the signs of the Kingdom.

Who should practise divine healing?

The plain answer is "anyone who believes". All God's people can pray for the sick, and should be encouraged to do so. Some people, however, will be given the gifts of healing, which means they will have a special anointing to heal. Paul asks the question in 1 Corinthians 12:30, "Do all have gifts of healing?" The question implies the answer "no". But we do need to qualify this blanket answer in the light of the New Testament and personal experience. Simon Magus in Acts 8 had charisma, and was probably healing the sick. Yet one can't see Peter including him in his healing team until he repented!

Then in Acts 19 there is the incident of the seven Jewish exorcists who were invoking the name of Jesus for healing, and got into serious trouble as a result.

We need to be sensitive to the work of healing in the Church. If wrongly developed it can cause harm to people. And since not everyone has the gift, those who are involved should be carefully screened. Most churches have trained teams of people, so that this sort of care can be exercised.

What means should we use?

In spite of the fact that faith is the key factor, means do play their part also. Jesus used mud and saliva to heal a man who was born blind (John 9:6). The centurion, on the other hand, said to Jesus " 'say the word and my servant will be healed' " (Luke 7:7), and the Lord did not even go to this man's bedside. Jesus was never averse to helping people's faith through means, and neither should we be.

Another example in the New Testament is the use of oil in James 5:14. Oil was used often in the Old Testament for ceremonial purposes, and in the recognising of ministries. We should use it too when it is appropriate.

Finally, there is the laying on of hands practised on many occasions by Jesus Christ, and later by the apostles. In Mark 16:18 it is specifically mentioned as one of the signs which would accompany those who believe.

Signs are a needed help to faith. God knows that we need them. The centurion's faith was strong; for him a word was enough. But God does not insist on this standard for all. He wants to help us to believe. We should seek to do the same by helping others, and particularly through the power of human touch.

What does God heal today?

If a person believes in the power of God to heal, then nothing is beyond his ability. Jesus' healings cover a wide range of sicknesses. Some years ago I heard about leg lengthening, and I have to confess laughed at it. But I have been forced to take it seriously, as I have witnessed the results.

There may be some false claims made, and some naïve

expectations. But leg lengthening widens the scope of healing enormously, and has the added advantage that one can actually see it taking place, which is not possible with many other forms of healing.

We must not put any limit on the grace and power of God. All demons are subject to His name, and all sicknesses *can* be healed, for there is no limit to God's power. The limitations are either in His will, which is not always to heal, or our faithlessness and disobedience.

10

IT'S A MIRACLE!

In October 1987 a hurricane swept the South of England causing major damage to trees and property. A few days afterwards I was having my hair cut when my barber said, "It's a miracle!" It is the sort of remark I would not have expected from him. So I asked him to tell me what the miracle was. He then told me how in the Sussex town where he lives many trees had come down, but none had hit any houses or injured any people.

There were some Christians who interpreted this natural disaster in terms of the judgment of God. Another way of seeing it was as a remarkable deliverance. The damage was immense, but casualties were very few. The storm occurred in the early hours of the morning. If it had come at almost any other time of the day or night, the casualties would have been heavy. On this occasion I prefer to see it as an example of the mercy of God rather than His judgment.

When we begin to think about the "gift of miracles" we are bound to consider the powers of nature and who controls them. It is an awesome subject, as the disciples found out on the lake when their boat nearly sank. "Even the wind and the waves obey him!" they said (Mark 4:41). Some claimed that the fire damage to York Minster was an act of retribution against the Bishop of Durham, who had been consecrated there the day before. Some have a morbid habit of picking on natural disasters, or train and plane crashes. They then attribute them either directly to God or indirectly by arguing

"God has removed his protection". The debate about "miracles" is as alive as ever.

In 1 Corinthians 12:10, Paul lists among the gifts of the Holy Spirit, "miraculous powers". We presume he believed that in the Church at Corinth there were church members who had a gift to perform miracles. Later on he asks the question, "Do all work miracles?" (v. 29). Again we presume he thought that some did, otherwise why ask the question? On the other hand because he asks the question we must assume that not all church members will have it.

We have to assume also that there is a difference between "the gifts of healing" and "working miracles". They are not the same, but overlap. I would suggest that some healings may be described as "miracles". Much healing can be the speeding up or re-timing of the natural ability of the body to heal itself. As we have seen we have a wonderful immunity system that deals with sickness, though it sometimes takes a long time. Through the gift of healing this can be accelerated.

But what happens when that system breaks down, as in the modern disease of Aids? In 1988 I heard of the first case of Aids being healed through prayer. That I would call a miracle. The New Testament takes the same line, because there is no known cure for this disease. For instance, when the lame man was healed in Jerusalem (Acts 3), the rulers and elders called it "an outstanding miracle" (Acts 4:16). Another example would be the raising of Lazarus from the dead by Jesus, which was more than a delayed healing, it was a notable miracle (John 11:38–44).

Perhaps the most significant miracles in the Old and New Testaments were those in which there was a divine act affecting nature itself. Thus locusts and quails are provided just when they are needed (Exodus 10:13–19 and 16:13). It is sometimes difficult to prove that a certain event is divinely caused. It could just have happened, or been a coincidence. Cecil Cousen writes, "miracles can both just happen and be made to happen".[5] It could I suppose be argued that Daniel hypnotised the lions in their den (Daniel 6:16–23), but we cannot put forward the same argument when we read of the three young men who were not so much as singed in Nebuchadnezzar's holocaust (Daniel 3:19–27).

When we come to the New Testament we read of outstanding miracles that Jesus performed, notably the feeding of the four thousand and five thousand, and His walking on the water. Clever attempts to explain these have been made by liberal theologians, such as the sandbank theory. This explains that Jesus walked on a narrow spit of land jutting out in the lake. The person of faith does not have to explain away such miracles. If Jesus is the Son of God and was involved with the Father in the creation of the universe, we should expect Him to control that creation. The natural world is not a closed system. God is not locked out of it. He has the power and authority to intervene so that His purposes may be achieved.

It follows that if we are the children of God, then we too can be involved with Him in miracles. We can see this in the Acts of the Apostles. People are healed when the shadow of Peter passes over them (Acts 5:15–16), something that never happened even in Jesus' ministry. In Acts 19:11 Luke tells us that "God did extraordinary miracles through Paul."

The reason for miracles

Miracles are primarily for the glory of God. When the disciples discussed with Jesus the reason why a man was born blind, they thought it was due either to the sin of the man or his parents (John 9). In this case Jesus said that sin was not necessarily involved. It was that "the work of God might be displayed in his life" (John 9:3). We can say, therefore, that miracles are not given by God for our enjoyment, but for His glory.

But secondly, we can say that miracles are for the safety, protection, provision and deliverance of the people of God. There are many examples in the Old Testament. Elijah is fed by the ravens, the walls of Jericho fall down, David is protected from murderous plots of Saul, and Daniel from the lions' claws. Hebrews 11 lists some of these rescue operations, but also records those who were martyred for their faith. In the New Testament similar deliverances take place, which we can call miracles. Peter is released from prison, and Paul is saved from drowning in the seas off Malta. Jesus Himself escaped from his assassins until the time appointed by the Father, when He submitted to His enemies and died for our sakes. We need to strike a balance. God does not always intervene in a miraculous way. Sometimes He allows His people to suffer loss, even of their own lives, to fulfil His purposes.

Miracles are often seen as deliverance from Satan and demonic attack. In the story of Moses's encounter with the magicians of Egypt we learn that Satan has the power to do miracles (Exodus 7-9). He can also use them against the people of God. A similar story is found in Acts 8. Philip begins to evangelise in Samaria. Simon Magus has been there before, amazing the crowds with a display of magic. But Philip was even more successful with miracles centered on Christ.

About ten years ago I nearly drowned in Lake Taupo in New Zealand while sailing solo. As a strong wind hit my boat and it keeled over I was immediately aware of the power of the enemy. Satan is descirbed as a "murderer" (John 8:44). I remember both crying to the Lord and against Satan as I was pulled under the icy waters of the lake. Fortunately, I was rescued. We never know when we will be in danger. Not even the Met Office forecast the hurricane in October 1987. But the Lord is the deliverer of His people, and He uses miracles sometimes to achieve His goals. The powers of nature ultimately serve the Lord not the enemy.

We all need to believe much more in a miracle-working God. It is a test of a true disciple. The Church is always in danger when it doubts the power of God to intervene in its affairs. Of course there is always the danger of superstition. Magic is not the same thing as miracles. But we must not allow ourselves to be ruled by scientific data. The Lord has a way of confounding the scientists.

11

GOD SPEAKS TODAY

Archbishop George Browne of Liberia once challenged the Province of West Africa with the words, "God is speaking, are we listening?" In the West we need to respond to these words even more. We are being drowned in words spoken and written, but are we hearing the Lord? In this chapter we are going to look at the gift of prophecy. This was highly rated by Paul. He wanted his readers to covet all the spiritual gifts, but adds, "especially the gift of prophecy" (1 Corinthians 14:1).

A few years ago I was preaching in a Lutheran Church in Strasbourg. It was Reformation Sunday. I reflected on a new kind of Reformation sweeping the world Church and told the congregation that if the first one hinged on the priesthood of all believers, then this one sprang from a fresh experience of the "prophethood" of all believers. In the sixteenth century the sale of papal indulgences was clearly a scandal. It only seemed possible to buy your forgiveness. The Reformers claimed again the right to have personal access to God, and His free pardon. The way had been blocked by tradition and human greed and skulduggery.

If the old Reformation opened the way *to God*, the new Reformation is opening the way *from God*. It is reminding the Church that Pentecost fulfilled for the whole Church the promise of Joel, " 'they will prophesy' " (Acts 2:18). Joel makes clear that there will be no generation gap. Both young and old will be open to God, and will hear and see Him. There will be no sex discrimination either. It will be " 'sons and daughters' " who will prophesy. Social and race barriers will go when the Holy Spirit is poured out. "Servants" will benefit as well as "masters", as on the day of Pentecost when a multiracial crowd was swept into the Kingdom. "Prophethood" is as much the will of God for all His people as priesthood.

I have called this chapter "God speaks today". I would emphasise the word "today", for that is where the charismatic element comes in. All would be agreed that God has spoken in the past. The epistle to the Hebrews says just that. "In the past God spoke to our forefathers through the prophets" (Hebrews 1:1). Equally there would be agreement that God has spoken to us uniquely in His Son, the "Word made flesh". Hebrews says the same, "in these last days he has spoken to us by his Son" (v. 2). Many would concur that the Bible is the revelation of God's truth to us in a way that no other writing can ever be. But does God still speak? Is the gift of prophecy still available? Does God still reveal Himself today, or is the Bible His final word? I believe God does still speak today through various means, one of which is the gift of prophecy and there should always be a ministry of prophets in the Church.

Radicals in the Church have asserted this for a long time, and people like the late Martin Luther King, Archbishop Desmond Tutu, Dietrich Bonhoeffer and a host of others have been hailed as "prophets". But the radicals' agenda is too narrow. The Charismatic Movement has an agenda which is wider and more comprehensive. It is calling the Church and the world to repentance and faith. To politicise the Gospel is to rob it of its unique power.

It is sad that Liberation Theology and the Charismatic Movement have few points of contact in Latin America, where they both have many followers. Most of the charismatics there are committed to social action. But Liberation Theology misses the point of the new Reformation, which is the release of spiritual gifts for all people. That is why in Latin America the Pentecostal/Charismatic Churches are "the haven of the masses", and people are flocking to them. Prophecy is for people not politics. It is right that Christians should take their full share in all aspects of national life including politics. Prophetic gifts may be expected in these areas too. But we should not assume that radical political and social opinions are in and of themselves true prophecy.

From the beginning God has spoken. Prophecy, therefore, has played a major part, because it has always been one of the main ways in which God has communicated to His people. Larry Christenson defines it as "the proclamation of a divinely inspired message". In the Old Testament the prophets are more often than not cast in the role of an unofficial opposition party, aloof from the "establishment" and called upon normally to say uncomplimentary things about it.

With the coming of Jesus Christ the style of prophecy changes. John the Baptist is the last of the old style prophets, Jesus the first of the new. The old prophets, like John the Baptist himself, lived separately from society. People had to go into the desert to hear them. Apart from Jeremiah they seldom appeared publicly in society. But Jesus prophesied from within society. All three in the end were put to death by the government of the day in order to silence them.

Prophecy plays a key role in the growth and development of the Church after Pentecost. Acts 13 is pivotal. The most vital apostolic ministry was about to be launched. We are told that the Church in Antioch had prophets as well as teachers. While fasting, and in the middle of a praise meeting, the Holy Spirit said, " 'Set apart for me Barnabas and Saul for the work to which I have called them' " (Acts 13:2). Here we see the prophetic gift playing a crucial part in the directing of the Church's outreach.

The key to a prophetic ministry is the art of listening. A prophet knows how to hear God speaking. In the classic story of Samuel's call to be a prophet, Eli teaches him to say, " 'Speak, LORD, for your servant is listening' " (1 Samuel 3:9). Our age tends to be short of prophecy because we are not good at listening. Words pour out, but the divine inspiration is often missing.

Let me give an example of the place that prophecy has played in my life. Some years ago I met a man called Dick Mills who had memorised thousands of scriptures. He would pray and then give people texts which he believed were relevant to them. I have kept several of these in my Bible. They have been an immense help to me. Or to give another example several people pray reguarly for me, and one of them is an elderly woman. When she prays she asks the Lord if there is anything He wants to say to me. She receives it, and then sends it to me. Some of these letters are in my Bible also. With the uncanniness of a true prophet she seems to know unerringly what and when I need to hear something from God.

I have heard some prophecies that are trite and unedifying. They said nothing very much, and I would have benefited more from a well-thought-out and prepared sermon. But amongst the thousands I have now heard there are more than a few which have been important to me. I have benefited enormously from them. Of course, some of the ones that have meant nothing to me could well have been vital for others who heard them. I would not want to judge that.

Questions about the gift

Where can prophecy be given?

Virtually anywhere. It can be included in preaching or teaching. It can come in a one-to-one counselling situation. It can be brought in public worship. It can be written in letters or books. In fact, it can be given to us in any situation where there is an opportunity for us to speak or write.

Who can prophesy?

All Christians can. The prophecy of Joel, fulfilled at Pentecost, says that the gift will be given to young and old, men and women, slaves and free (Acts 2:17-21). The gift has been known sometimes to be given to unbelievers. This was true of Balaam in the Old Testament, who was an evil occultist (Numbers 22-24).

Can we prophesy during a Sunday service?

There is no reason why such a gift should not be shared in divine service. It will depend on the state of the church whether the gift will be received or not. It would be better not to prophesy if either the minister or the congregation would not accept it. Some churches have such a strict kind of service, there may not be room provided for this gift. The church, not you, will be the loser.

Can provision be organised by the church for such a gift?

Yes. Our experience at large conferences is that it is best to gather a "word gift group" together, who are known to have the gift, are in good standing in the church, and know when to speak and when to be silent. The local church could easily set such a group apart to serve it in this way. If the building is large, it may well be necessary to see that a microphone is near at hand, and the minister can fix an appropriate time during the service when the group can make their contribution.

Should we accept all prophecies?

Certainly not! They can be of the flesh (human) or demonic, so care needs to be taken. In 1 Corinthians 14:29 Paul says that the rest of the church should "weigh" the prophecies after they have been given. This means to discern their source and their content.

This should not be seen only in a negative sense. The weighing is primarily to apply them concretely to the church situation or individuals within the church. It is to be recommended that people take notes as the words come, so that the messages are not forgotten. Later it may be possible to weigh them even more carefully.

Do prophecies impart guidance?

They certainly did in the Acts of the Apostles. As we have already seen, it was a prophecy in the Church at Antioch that guided the Church to send out Paul and Barnabas on their first missionary journey (Acts 13:1).

But it can be abused. One should be sceptical of proposals of marriage or a word to part with money which comes through prophecy. Guidance in prophecy should be tested carefully, and there should usually be confirmation from some other quarter.

How should we regard prophecies which brings judgment?

With a good deal of scepticism. Generally prophecy is for "strengthening, encouragement and comfort" (1 Corinthians 14:3). However, this sometimes does include rebukes or criticisms. They can arrest God's people when they are going wrong, and they can redirect them into the right paths. But judgmental words are not the way the Holy Spirit normally works.

As in all aspects of church life, each member needs to be in submission to the whole Body of Christ. The leadership established in the local church should be respected. No one should feel free to prophesy unless they are at the same time prepared to submit their words to the larger body. If this rule is kept, peace will reign, and the church will be edified.

12

OUR SPIRITUAL RADAR

The seventh gift listed by Paul is called "distinguishing between spirits". It brings us to a nasty subject. Anyone who knows anything about it will tell you how revolting it can be. Satanic power when it is incarnated in human beings can plumb depths of shame which at times are hard to imagine. It does point us to a tough ministry. We should all be grateful to God that He has given us weapons to deal with such evils.

Some years ago a film called *The Exorcist* proved very popular. It made people aware of the horror of demonic power, and our weakness against it. Medical means are useless. Only God's weapons are proof against it. Some time ago I met a police officer who before he retired was detailed to handle the criminal aspects of witchcraft and satanism. It was only his faith that kept him sane.

But what does this gift "distinguish"? First of all we need to beware of what has been called "dualism". Those who hold to this divide the world and what happens in it into two kingdoms, God's and Satan's. Thus all that happens or is said is either from God or Satan. Such thinking is deceptive because it does not account for the human will and spirit which can function independently of both God and Satan. It is not right to reckon on the basis that all that is not of God is Satanic. God created man in His image and gave him his freedom. This, however, does not mask the fact that we are on a battlefield in which God's will and Satan's are in conflict.

So the gift of distinguishing spirits gives us suitable weapons in the arena of Satanic power. It helps us to know about these forces and how to defeat them. It enables us to release people held captive by them. We are also able to distinguish between what is of God and what is merely human. The human spirit is not an evil spirit, though capable of being taken over by one. We need to know what is of God, what is human, and what is demonic. Our response will differ according to that discernment.

When we compare our day and that of the apostles, it is sad to see our ignorance of Satanic power. The apostles were vividly aware that the battle was primarily spiritual. "Our struggle is not against flesh and blood," Paul writes, "but against the rulers, against the authorities, against the powers of this dark world and against the spiritual forces of evil in the heavenly realms" (Ephesians 6:12). Today we have been so subjected to human ideas and a secular worldview that we deny all this. We interpret these passages as referring to secular structures, like multinational companies. *In my view there is more evidence of Satanic power in the Western Church than in the Third World. So Satan, who delights to masquerade as "an angel of light" confuses and distorts this truth.* Demonic power may be sophisticated in the West, but it is no less real. In fact it is more dangerous to encounter the Devil as an angel of light.

We shall get nowhere until we recognise these powers as real. Of course we hear lots of talk which denies, or even laughs at what I have written. It ignores or minimises the influence of demonic forces. On the other hand we should also recognise that there have been people who have exaggerated the work of the enemy, to Satan's advantage. But times have not changed since the apostles were living. The enemy is just as active today as he was in Bible times. Indeed he is all the more so as he sees that "his time is short". Spiritual radar is vital to track him down, and find out what he is doing. Then we can do battle with his forces until they are overcome and their slaves released.

From my own fairly limited experience there are four main doors through which the enemy slips into our lives. This may happen unawares. He then controls areas of our lives, and so hinders us from doing our best for the Lord. The ones I'm listing are all areas where we are most vulnerable in the West.

1. Drugs and alcohol

Anything which takes over control of our lives is a danger to us. Drugs and alcohol destroy people's lives today more than any other agency. When we hand over some part of our humanity, we openly invite the enemy to move in. He is not slow to exploit the situation for his own ends. Drinking a lot of alcohol and using drugs nearly always lead to violence. This also is a symptom of demonic power.

2. The occult

Another door-opener for evil spirits is dabbling in the occult. There has been a major growth of occult practices throughout the Western world in the last twenty years. In the Third World primitive animism, spiritualism and idol worship are still rife. One third of Tanzanians, for example, are still animistic. Those who witness amongst them say that a ministry like this, which relies heavily on the ability to "distinguish spirits", is necessary to set them free and enable them to come to Christ. The same is true in many Latin American countries, as, for instance, Brazil, where spiritualism is almost the state religion.

Many in the West, and even some Christians, are dabblers in black arts. Perhaps because of a spiritual vacuum, black magic, séances, yoga and Eastern mysticism are constantly being explored. People do not realise how dangerous these are. They need to repent and be set free so that they can confess that Jesus is Lord. Then they are able to live an effective Christian life.

3.   Sexual sins and perversions

We have lived through a period when almost anything goes
as regards sexual behaviour. The "swinging Sixties"
ushered in a time of moral permissiveness. People thought
that everything was all right provided you enjoyed it and
did it "in love". Thousands sought pleasure and release
in sexual perversions and pornography. Instead they were
trapped by Satan. Often when a person is found to be
harassed or invaded by evil spirits, the cause is sexual
licence, promiscuity, homosexual practices, or other
perversions. By no means all homosexuality is satanically
caused. But it can be due at least in part to satanic power.

4.   Child abuse

We have heard a lot about child abuse recently, and it is
a major social factor in the West. Large numbers of children
grow up in homes where they have to contend with violence,
drunkenness, blasphemy, sex abuse, and bad language. It
is no surprise that many crack. It is fertile ground for the
invasion of evil spirits.

This raises the question, "Can Christians be possessed by evil
spirits?" The answer is "yes" and "no", depending on what
you mean by "possession". It is plainly not possible for
Christians, who have the Holy Spirit dwelling in them, to be
taken over entirely or "possessed" by Satan, unless they hand
over full control to him, which is unlikely. But, as we have
seen, it is possible for doors to be left open, and for the
influence of demons to invade a person's life, even though
they are Christians. And when this happens early in life, the
power may not be dealt with either in baptism or through
personal faith in Christ. We have been passing through a time
of superficial faith. People have made shallow professions.
Certainly I have been involved in scores of cases of genuine
Christians who have needed to be set free from such forces.

This gift is important in the whole area of the activity of demons. But this is not its only use. There is also, as we have seen, a need to distinguish between the Holy Spirit and the human spirit. A weakness of Christians is false piety. So the person with this gift will be able to tell quickly whether there is sincerity in what a person says or does. Peter had this gift when he dealt with Ananias and Sapphira (Acts 5:1 – 11). This married couple told lies about the money they had given to the Church. The sin of hypocrisy is not far from any of us if we are Church members. Those who profess most are closest to it. So the ability to discern the truth is important for the building of trust in the Christian community.

It was not until I was baptised in the Spirit that I started to experience this whole dimension. I became vividly aware of spiritual warfare. Many incidents over the years have taught me this is a real world. Both Jesus and the apostles came up against these forces whenever they preached the Kingdom. There were constant power encounters between the Holy Spirit and evil spirits. It was like stirring up hornets' nests.

Because of the dangers involved, some Church leaders have tried to limit those involved in this work. This can be a short-sighted policy. What is needed is more people and better training. Every minister and many lay people should be taught how to set people free from demonic power. There do need to be limits. Some people may well be unsuitable. Like cigarette packets, there should be a health hazard warning written across this ministry.

However, the gift has been given to the Body of Christ. Let's accept it gladly, and use it to uncover the ploys of the enemy and defeat him.

13

NEW LANGUAGES

It has sometimes been said that because "speaking in tongues" comes last in Paul's list of gifts in 1 Corinthians 12:10 it is the least important. Such is the stuff of prejudice! We might just as well conclude that "love" is the least of the Christian graces because Paul lists it after faith and hope. Actually he rates it "the greatest" (1 Corinthians 13:13). For Paul the value of the gifts depends on their function not the order in which he places them, unless he specifies it.

I am linking together the two gifts of "speaking in different kinds of tongues" and that of "the interpretation of tongues" in this chapter and the next. In this one we shall look at the nature of these gifts, and in the next, how they should operate in the life of the Church and the individual.

Dennis Bennett once wrote, "Speaking in tongues is not a feat of the intelligence, but it is the most intelligent thing I've ever done." It has been the most controversial of the gifts, because it challenges the over-active cleverness of Christians in the West. It also exposes the cold and impersonal nature of much formal worship. Twenty years ago, speaking in tongues was frowned on when it first began to be practised widely in the Anglican and other historic churches. It no longer excites attention. The novelty seems to have worn off. This is not because it is no longer practised; far from it. It is because Charismatics have largely won the arguments. At the same time there has been a maturing process in the Charismatic Renewal. A wider range of gifts are being experienced. As a result speaking in tongues is no longer being majored on. The gift does not downgrade the intellect. It does not promote what one evangelical leader once called "mindless Christianity". But it does recognise that the mind has its own limits. In other words the Spirit is using tongues to restore a balance. He wants to set the Church free from being locked into a system of thought which closes the mind to the inspiration of the Holy Spirit.

Larry Christenson has described speaking in tongues as a gift which "alerts us to the reality of God . . . an unparalleled experience of God's presence." In 1 Corinthians 14 Paul spends more time describing this gift than any other. But first we need to establish the link between this gift and the occurrences in the Acts of the Apostles. At Pentecost, in the house of Cornelius, and when Paul prayed for the Ephesian disciples, the coming of the Spirit was evidenced by speaking in tongues. In other words, the pattern of Pentecost was repeated.

Some have argued that the speaking in tongues at Pentecost was different from that described by Paul in 1 Corinthians. In fact they were exactly the same. The only difference lies in the circumstances. At Pentecost the gift was given at the moment when the disciples were baptised in the Spirit, and the audience were unbelievers. The languages were unknown to those who spoke them, but recognised by those who heard them. For the listeners, therefore, the tongues took on the form of prophecy and a sign, thus fulfilling the words of Joel " 'they will prophesy' " (Acts 2:18). On the other hand in the Church in Corinth the gift, in its normal use in church worship, was in languages unknown both to speakers and listeners, hence the command to have "interpretation".

Speaking in tongues: the basics

1. It is speaking to God (1 Corinthians 14:2)

It is a prayer language; a way of communicating more effectively with God. Our age, with radios and televisions, telephones, teleprinters and fax machines has developed rapid and effective means of communication. But at the basic human level we are as bad as ever. Husbands and wives often drift apart because of their difficulties in sharing together. The same is true between parents and children. When it comes to communicating with God, we are worse than our forefathers. Maybe this is one of the main reasons why the Holy Spirit has chosen our generation to restore this gift to us.

2.   It is speaking mysteries in the Spirit (v.2)

This is the hardest part to understand for our age is primarily interested in facts and figures, like the *Financial Times* share index and the latest MORI (Market and Opinion Research Institute) poll. It does not appreciate "mysteries", for there must be a reason for everything. All we say and do must be rationally based. We are not open to surprises, and we have to justify with our minds everything we are involved in. No wonder this gift is viewed with such scepticism! Perhaps we need to appreciate more the spiritual life of the Eastern Orthodox Churches. For them "mystery" holds an important place in the way they understand God and their relationship with Him. The typical Western approach says that everything we say and do must be "meaningful", to use a modern cliché. Not so with the Orthodox.

3.   It is self-edifying (v. 4)

Modern Western man finds it hard to believe that speaking unknown words to God can possibly be edifying. "Surely we should know what we are saying" is the response. All one can say is "try it and see". I can still remember today the moments when I first used this gift, and the immediate awareness I had that I was being edified. This is one of the most important reasons why the gift needs to be used regularly in private prayer. It is not a waste of time. Far from it, it strengthens and encourages us.

4.   It is praying with the spirit (v. 14–15)

Here Paul contrasts two ways of praying – with the mind and with the spirit. He commends both. He tells us that when we pray in tongues, "the mind is unfruitful." Literally this means "lies fallow", like a field that is temporarily not producing crops. Speaking in tongues is a form of exercising our spiritual faculties, those areas of our humanity where the gifts of the Spirit freely function. Secular life ignores this side of our nature, and much church life does too. The gifts of the Spirit operate at the level of our spirit, not our mind.

5.   It is a sign (v. 22)

As we have seen, speaking in tongues at Pentecost was a sign that the Holy Spirit had come. The Pentecostal age had arrived and Joel had predicted it. Many Pentecostals call this "the initial evidence". It assured the Christians that Jesus was still with them. It convinced them that God had given them the power of the Holy Spirit. It was to be used as evidence to help convince the unbelievers who heard it, that God was there in reality. In other words it was a sign and wonder to unbelievers. It caught their attention and prompted them to ask the right kind of questions. It led to their hearing the Gospel, and at least three thousand of them being converted and baptised.

Speaking in tongues is sometimes recognised as a known language, although not known to the speaker. I once spoke in tongues in Cambridge and the words I spoke were interpreted. Apparently I had spoken a Central African language, and the interpretation was a close rendering of what I had just said. There are other proven cases of this use of speaking in tongues. It can be a sign as well as a personal blessing.

It can also be a sign to the Church. An example of this is in Acts 10. Peter preached under divine orders to Cornelius and his friends. Suddenly the Holy Spirit fell on them, even before Peter had finished his address. How did they know it was another Pentecost? The evidence was the speaking in tongues. We are told that those who had come with Peter were amazed that the Gentiles had received the Spirit, "For they heard them speaking in tongues and praising God" (v. 46).

Gone are the days when all we ever heard about this gift was from scholars who wrote learned tomes about what they called "glossolalia". This gift has again taken its rightful place in the life of individuals. It is seldom heard in public, and then it is always "interpreted". We shall be discussing that gift in the next chapter and looking at how the gift of tongues and the gift of interpretation operate in public especially in worship services.

14

TONGUES IN ACTION

In an article called "Avoiding Extremes", Father Tom Forrest, a Roman Catholic priest, writes, "Jesus wants us to have a vocabulary of praise carrying us beyond our own weak words, but he does not want tongues to be the only way we pray, or to be a completely undisciplined style of prayer that we use to prove ourselves superior to those who may lack this gift, but perhaps enjoy a far greater gift of only speaking words of love." Paul handled the tongues issue in Corinth in the same way. He seeks to drive a path between the two extremes of using tongues for personal showing off and selfish ends on the one hand, and forbidding it altogether on the other (1 Corinthians 14:39).

There really is no excuse for the misuse of this gift, since Paul lays down clearly how it should operate. A key to help us understand it, is to distinguish between the private and public use of the gift. This is implicit in 1 Corinthians 14:1-40. For instance, Paul thanks God that he speaks in tongues more than they did. But he goes on to say that in the church he would rather speak in words people could understand than in tongues (v. 18-19). If he spoke in tongues so much, and didn't do it in church, we must presume he did so in private. David du Plessis once said that because Paul prayed ten thousand words in tongues privately, his few words in public were dynamic.

In the short history of the Charismatic Renewal speaking in tongues has become rare in public, but continues to be a vital expression of prayer in private.

Gifted People

Paul is insistent that when someone delivers a message in tongues in public his words should be interpreted (v. 27-28). There is a simple reason for this — the need to edify. If people do not understand what is being said, they will not be edified, even if the speaker is. Paul lays it even more firmly on the line. He urges that speakers in tongues should pray that the gift to interpret be given either to them or to another person (v. 13).

In verse 15 Paul mentions singing with the spirit. This is a choral version of speaking in tongues. Here the Holy Spirit inspires both words and music at the same time. I shall never forget the first time I heard singing in tongues. It was at an Elim conference in the Sixties. It was Heaven on earth. When a body of people do this there is no need to interpret it, since it is edifying in itself. It is also a marvellous way of expressing unity.

The Roman Catholic Church still finds Latin a useful language of unity. In the Early Church speaking in tongues played a similar role, since it transcended all languages. Sometimes people say that speaking in tongues is divisive. It can be when improperly used. But when used as the Spirit intends, it has a useful role in uniting people.

But how does speaking in tongues compare with prophecy? Paul is concerned to interest the Corinthians in prophecy more than tongues. Thus he urges them to seek the gifts of the Spirit "especially the gift of prophecy" (v. 1). He then compares the two gifts and tries to show why prophecy is superior. Tongues is speaking to God, while prophecy is to people (v. 2-3). Tongues edifies the individual, whereas prophecy edifies the church (v. 4). But what happens if there is interpretation of tongues? It would seem that tongues together with interpretation in Paul's eyes are equal to prophecy. They raise the value and importance of tongues to the level of prophecy (v. 5).

The interpretation of tongues

What then is the gift of interpreting tongues? Clearly it is not the ability to translate it. There is a world of difference between translating and interpreting. No, it is another gift of the Holy Spirit. It is not the natural gift of translating a known language. It is the ability to put into a known language what has just been said in an unknown language. A question naturally arises from this. Why have speaking in tongues and interpretation of tongues when prophecy can bring the same message? Isn't speaking in tongues unnecessary?

There are a number of answers one can give to this. First, there is a value in speaking in tongues preceding the interpretation, even if it could have come directly in a prophecy. For tongues can act like a herald or the old town crier. It commands attention, and everyone is waiting and listening for the words to be interpreted.

But there is another reason which is often overlooked. According to Paul tongues is uttering mysteries with the spirit (v. 2). Its main use is speaking to God in prayer and worship. So surely the interpretation will have the same purpose. But prophecy has a different focus and object altogether. Through it God speaks to His people with an up-to-date and relevant message. Thus we should expect the interpretation to be mainly an expression of prayer or worship and, therefore, different from a prophecy.

I have known many occasions when the level of faith drops and worship flags. Tongues and interpretation together arrest the situation. They make sure that God's word is heard. The situation changes, and people are back under the anointing of the Holy Spirit, alert and listening.

Principles of public worship

The Church should always be thankful for the Charismatics in Corinth, and for their sometimes bizarre behaviour. If they

had been a model church we would not have had
1 Corinthians 12-14! And imagine the New Testament
without 1 Corinthians 13! We learn more about the worship
of the early Christians from these chapters than from the whole
of the rest of the New Testament. Paul lays down some simple
rules which we would be well advised to follow in our own
worship.

1. Everything should be in love

The motive of all we do and say, when together as the body of
Christ, should be love. In 1 Corinthians 13:1 Paul says that
worship without love will be "only a resounding gong or a
clanging cymbal". In all things we are to "Follow the way of love"
(1 Corinthians 14:1).

2. Everything should be under control

Paul says that "The spirits of prophets are subject to the control
of prophets. For God is not a God of disorder but of peace" (1
Corinthians 14:32-33). We should be suspicious of anyone who
says, "I was compelled to speak". Compulsion usually comes
from Satan. Self-control is of God not Satan, and is one of the
fruits of the Spirit (Galatians 5:23).

Some people think that disorder is a sign of the presence
of the Spirit. It is nothing of the kind. Equally false is the
idea that orderly and musically correct worship is of itself
pleasing to the Lord. Frankly He hates some of it. The prophet
Amos railed against it in his day. " 'I hate, I despise your
religious feasts' " (Amos 5:21). And " 'Away with the noise
of your songs! I will not listen to the music of your harps' "
(Amos 5:23). This was strong medicine for the choir master
or organist to take!

It is God's order, not the human kind that counts. The two

are quite different. The best worship will always have a balance between the spontaneous and the prepared, the liturgical and the free. There is a place for preparing it, and also for letting it run free.

3. Everything should be edifying

Paul writes, ''All of these must be done for the strengthening of the church'' (1 Corinthians 14:26). This is the overriding consideration for Paul, and the reason he wanted to outlaw the solo speaker in tongues in church. But we need to extend this principle to every part of worship. Some aspects of modern worship should be dropped because they are unedifying. This applies to the shallow words of some popular songs. Also to sermons more intended to please than to edify.

4. Everything should be orderly

Paul ends his teaching on worship with the words, ''But everything should be done in a fitting and orderly way'' (1 Corinthians 14:40). Some people deduce from this that he was thinking of Anglican Mattins and the *Book of Common Prayer*. Perish the thought! The most orderly place in most towns and cities is the cemetery! Alas some worship is like that, orderly but dead. The order Paul had in mind was the order of the Holy Spirit. This allows the free but responsible flow of charismatic gifts. And all this should interweave with the richness of the Church's liturgies. We can and should have the best of both worlds.

15

LETTING GO AND LETTING GOD

There is something in us which finds it hard to let go. Yet if God is to have His way in our lives and in the Church we have to be prepared to take a few risks. As we have seen, John Wimber has described faith as "taking risks". In the development of his Vineyard Church in Southern California there was a long period when nothing much happened. They prayed for the sick, and the sick got worse. It was all very frustrating. They tried to let go, but God didn't seem to answer their prayers. It would have been easy for their critics to conclude that God was not in what they were doing. They were, however, taking the risk of exposure to ridicule as blatantly as Noah did when he built a large boat thousands of miles from the sea. "I told you it wouldn't work," no doubt their critics said. But the risk ultimately bore fruit. Hundreds were blessed and healed.

One is reminded of the story of the woman who came to Jesus asking Him to heal her daughter of an evil spirit (Matthew 15:21–28). Jesus couldn't have been less helpful. First of all, He ignored her altogether. She might have been talking to the stones. He then told her she didn't belong to the right race. Only Jews qualified. But the woman persisted. She would not be shaken off. She persisted until she got what she wanted, and was commended by Jesus for her faith. That is what real faith is. It lets go and lets God do what He wants. It may be God is silent and inactive. That's fine. But we don't leave it like that. We go on asking until we have received.

There is often a testing time both for people and churches. It lies between the first flush of excitement, and the start of a fruitful ministry. It is similar to the experience of Jesus between His baptism in Jordan, with the words of the Father ringing in His ears affirming Him as the Son of God, and the start of His public work. It is a season in the desert, when the Word of God and the promises in it are put to the test. Do we really believe them?

There are all kinds of religious activities which hinder the work of God in our lives. They can be substitutes for the real thing. We feel we have to "do something" for God. And if God isn't doing anything very much, then we step in and do it for Him. It then becomes something false, and it sullies our relationship with Him. Religious activism for its own sake can be a major hindrance in the Church today.

This is not to say that there is no place for human activity. But that activity needs to be done in obedience to the Lord. It should also be in His strength and for His glory. Nor am I saying that religious means are to be rejected altogether. But they should always be means to an end, never ends in themselves.

Much modern Christianity leaves the acts of God out altogether. Many would have to say if they were honest, "God has acted but now it is up to us to do His will." There is no allowance for His present-day acts. In other words we attempt to do to God what He did to Adam and Eve when He removed them from the garden. We do not let Him come and change things.

This is true of the way some people see the Word of God. For them the Bible is God's final word. He has been silent ever since. He is not allowed to address His people except through the words of the Bible. But this is actually a position of faithlessness! It removes from our armoury several of the gifts of the Spirit. I believe God does still speak through prophecy, as well as words of wisdom and knowledge.

It is equally true of the activity of God. Some see the death of Jesus, and His being raised from the dead as the final acts of

God. According to them it is as if God is now paralysed. He does not intervene any more in our lives. His hand is shortened. But such a view of God's activity is false. He does still act today. Things happen because He causes them to happen, and things change because He has chosen to change them. God is constantly in action, providing, protecting and healing the people of God. Our job is to make sure He is free to do this, and to recognise it when He does so.

New challenges

We shall have to face many challenges in the new world of the Spirit. So many things will have to change. Self-reliance has been drilled into us at home and school. "Standing on your own feet" is regarded as vital for existence. It is only when all else fails, that we try God. He is the last resort.

This attitude has to change. The promptings of the Spirit are gentle and quiet. He neither pushes nor shouts. The still small voice is not easy to hear against the cacophony of sounds which make up modern life. Our thought processes are determined by our education; we filter everything through "reason". So it takes courage and determination to literally "change our minds", and let the Holy Spirit speak to us.

We need to be serious about this. Miracles are unreasonable acts of God. They are disturbing because they seem to change the rules of life, and take away our security. Some see faith as the ultimate security. That is not true. Faith is a commitment to the unknown, and the willingness to allow God to suspend scientific certainties, if He chooses to.

Pride

One of the first casualties will be our human pride. When head knowledge rules supreme, then there is no room for the gifts of the Holy Spirit. However humble a person may seem to be, if that person shuts out the Holy Spirit and lets his rational processes reign supreme he is by definition a proud person. God hates human pride. It is the claim of a human being to rule in God's world without God. To be really committed to Jesus Christ means letting our minds become as putty, so that the Spirit can change and shape them. Many a Western Christian has handed over everything to the Lord, except his mind. It is revealing that when a person is baptised by immersion the last part to go under is the head. Alas, in many cases the head is never immersed in the Spirit.

We are living in a world which takes great pride in its scientific achievements. In the field of medical science, we are always about to discover the cure for something, and then Aids or Salmonella poisoning comes along, and man has no immediate answer. It will always be like that. This is why divine healing is so vital. It humbles our human pride.

We cannot function freely in the Spirit until we have really dealt with pride. I know it is possible to be proud of the gifts of the Spirit, or the divine power offered to us, and received by us. That too needs to be dealt with. But human pride more than anything else prevents us operating freely in the gifts of the Spirit. If we think we are clever or competent enough ourselves, then we have no need of such divine assistance.

Another aspect of pride is status. In our world professionals reign supreme. They have status. They have achieved success in one field or other. Their security is in their expertise, and so they steer their lives around that competence, so that their shortcomings in other areas will not be exposed. The Holy Spirit does not honour status. In the Kingdom of God there are no status symbols. That has to go with everything else.

Other securities

As we go through life we develop our own security systems, which protect us from danger, and give us easy answers to sometimes complex problems. It is inner fear which drives us to set up our alarm systems, and we squat nervously behind our protective walls, trusting in the system to warn us of any danger. The problem of such a scenario is that the system can easily cut out the Holy Spirit as well, and that is tragic. Yet Christians are called to live dangerously, and that will entail moving out from our protective screen so that we can respond freely to the Holy Spirit.

Fundamentalism is an obvious example of this, whether we are looking at the Muslim or Christian version of it. The Islamic Revolution in Iran is an extreme example. Here there is total intolerance. Iranians are not free to differ or to question what is put forward by the government. The walls are built high around the country to prevent contamination of its pure doctrines. But Christians have also built their walls and infallible systems.

One of my securities was evangelicalism. I soon discovered that the Holy Spirit is not a party spirit, in fact Paul calls that spirit one of the works of the flesh (Galatians 5:20 AV). So it had to go. I had to move away from those secure walls. They had, for example, kept me from accepting the gifts of the Spirit. The party line had usually been that the gifts were just for the apostles, and were removed from the Church after their deaths.

For others the security can be of a Catholic variety. Some of us grow up with a strictly traditional view of the Church, worship, prayer and the sacraments. Others follow Liberation Theology, or take a liberal view of the Bible and Christian doctrine. Liberals can be as defensive and selective about what they believe or don't believe as the most rabid fundamentalist. Such narrow and blinkered views will hinder us from hearing what the Holy Spirit is saying to the Churches.

What is true of churchmanship can also be true of politics. There is no stronger security alarm system than Marxism. Another is the rigid attitude of some radicals to South Africa. Bishop Bill Burnett, the former Archbishop of Cape Town, was a powerful opponent of apartheid in his country. Then he was baptised in the Holy Spirit. His whole fixed attitude to political questions changed. He continued his strong opposition to apartheid, but he saw there were other things which were part of the Kingdom of God which needed doing. He suddenly saw the importance of evangelism, something which most liberals in the Church entirely ignore. He saw that some of those who shouted loudest for justice in the world were committed to a narrow view of the Church, which is a kind of ecclesiastical apartheid.

We need to surrender all our carefully constructed systems to the Lord, if we are to hear clearly the Holy Spirit and be led in His ways. We must listen to God not man.

16

MIXING FRUIT AND GIFTS

We are to be good as well as to do good. According to Peter, the Lord Jesus Christ,

> went around doing good and healing all who were under the power of the devil, because God was with him (Acts 10:38).

The Son of God is the perfect example of a man who *was* good and *did* good. The two attributes were in perfect balance. They blended together and were in harmony throughout His life.

It is easy for our lives to be unbalanced, and somehow to get the blend wrong. It is quite common for some to criticise the behaviour of Charismatics, and for Charismatics to do the same to those whom they think lack power and spiritual gifts. It is no accident that in his letters Paul lists both the gifts and the fruit of the Spirit (1 Corinthians 12:1–11, Galatians 5:22–23). The fact that there are nine of each may be a coincidence, but both lists are evidence of the presence and power of the Holy Spirit. Both glorify Jesus Christ, for we are to seek to be like Him in what He was as well as in what He did.

The temptations of the powerful

In his famous book *Money, Sex and Power*, Richard Foster has helped us to see the main areas of human temptation.[6] Most people recognise the dangers which money and sex present to us. The disasters caused by the misuse of money and sex are self-evident. They are aspects of power in themselves. But the author has added "power" in its own right to the other two. "Power can destroy or create," he writes, and all will agree with him.

Charismatic gifts put power into our hands. They can make us rich. They can make us famous and popular. They also place people in our hands, and to use power over people wrongly is one of the hardest temptations to resist. Jesus had to face this, as well as the more physical temptations in His desert experience. When Satan offered Jesus the kingdoms of the world, their authority and splendour, he was offering a deal which would give Jesus supreme power over people.

I have watched Christians, after they are baptised in the Spirit, entering into a strong ministry, and then losing out because of pride. The power goes to their heads, and touches their hearts less and less. Power struggles are not unknown in the charismatic world, but they mar the image of Christ in our lives, and are a hindrance to our witness.

Paul had to face this problem in the Church at Corinth. Some have argued that 1 Corinthians 13, the chapter on love, is a put-down of spiritual gifts by Paul. No, it is a firm statement of the primacy of love in the exercise of the gifts. It is a plea for the joining together of the two not the sundering of them apart. It is impossible if we understand the real meaning of love to express it without gifts. Equally, it is wrong to substitute gifts for love. To be true and effective the gifts need to be used in love. Love should be the chief motive. It is because we love people, that we want to give them gifts. But to force gifts on people against their will is just as unloving.

The temptations of the powerless

There is a tendency these days to draw attention to the power of the rich and the powerlessness of the poor. Yet man is much more than an economic statistic, and it is wrong to assess people solely according to their incomes. There are many rich people who are powerless in terms of the Kingdom of God, and many poor, though not all, who are powerful in terms of the same Kingdom. God does not look on the outward appearance, nor what our bank balance may be. Rich and poor alike will be judged by God. In spite of what some people say, God does not have a bias towards the rich or the poor. The Gospel is for both. Neither the "Prosperity Gospel", nor the so-called preferential option for the poor, square with God's character of justice.

The major problem the spiritually powerless have to face is jealousy. It is hard for the "have-nots" to accept the "haves" when they possess more power and influence than they do. In Galatians Paul points out that the one born of the flesh persecuted the one "born by the power of the Spirit". He ruefully adds, "It is the same now" (Galatians 4:29). The most opposed and disliked section of the Church has always been the one born in revival. John Wesley was never popular in the Church of England, although he remained a lifelong member of it. The same is true of the Pentecostals, who until recently have been treated with disdain by the other Churches.

Finally, I want us to look at the fruit and the gifts of the Spirit together, and how they inter-relate and complement each other.

Love

In Peter's list of fruit, love comes last (2 Peter 1:7). Here it comes first. Just as fruit always tells us what the plant is, so true love tells us what the person is like. Paul uses the obscure Greek word, *agape*. The Greeks would have used the word *eros*, because it was commonly used at the time, and was about the most important word in the Greek language. If Paul had wanted to impress people, he would have chosen *eros* rather than *agape*. But the word is never used in the New Testament.

The authors seemed to have deliberately rejected it.

Agape became the favourite word of the New Testament writers. *Eros* described man's aspirations for God. It moves from earth up to heaven. But the word *agape* reverses the direction. It tells of God's commitment to us. It moves from heaven down to earth. True Christian love describes the feelings and desires implanted in a person to share what he has with a person who needs it. The motive for sharing these wonderful gifts should be love.

Joy

Love and joy seem to belong together. Charles Wesley blends the two words in his famous hymn "Love Divine". For in the next line, having sung about "Love Divine", we sing about "Joy of Heav'n". Love brings joy into the world, just as hatred and envy bring sadness.

We need to see these fruit as positive qualities. It is easy to define them in terms of absence rather than presence. Thus we sometimes think of joy as an absence of sadness. It is much more than that. Christian joy is something that pervades situations. It drives out gloom and despondency whatever the circumstances, and replaces them with happiness and hope. In the parable of the talents, the reward for being faithful is to " 'enter into the joy of your master' ", or as the NIV translates it, " 'Come and share your master's happiness.' " (Matthew 25:21). Heaven is a place where joy is all-pervasive. The Holy Spirit recreates this same joy in our hearts, though often in much less congenial conditions!

Whenever the gifts of the Spirit are around, there will be what Peter calls "inexpressible and glorious joy" (1 Peter 1:8).

Peace

I still remember the excitement in 1945 when the Second World War ended. Peace at last (or was it)? But we need to see that

God's peace is not just the absence of war. Peace is more than an armistice, a laying down of arms. In fact it is not primarily dependent on outward circumstances. It is something that comes from within our hearts, and spreads from there to other people, and can even affect places.

The Greek word *eirene* is a relationship word, like the other two words of this most famous of all triads. It means to join or bind people together. Many have laughed at the words in the old hymn, "Peace, perfect peace, with loved ones far away?". Sometimes peace does reign when our loved ones are away from us! But the test of true love, and the peace that comes with it, is when we are close to people. The fruit of the Spirit, and the power of the blood of Jesus Christ, make such peace possible. Paul describes this key concept in Ephesians, "For he himself is our peace, who has made the two one and has destroyed the barrier, the dividing wall of hostility . . . thus making peace . . . He came and preached peace to you who were far away and peace to those who were near" (Ephesians 2:14–17). Actually Paul has in mind racial peace in this passage. But whether it is racial, tribal, economic, class or Church, peace is a powerful expression of the ministry of the Holy Spirit.

The passage I have just quoted has been important in the work of the Christian Renewal centre in Rostrevor, Northern Ireland, which was founded in 1974 by the Rev. Cecil Kerr. For many years Roman Catholics and Protestants have lived together in this Centre with sectarian murders taking place all around them. They have been able to show by their lives that the peace of Jesus Christ can overcome the worst prejudices and fears.

Patience

I have a plate hanging in my study with the words inscribed on it, "Lord give me patience, but hurry!" The Greek word literally means "long-suffering". It is a quality which most people have little time for; we are always in too much of a hurry. I am thankful for all I have learnt from the Third World, where life without patience is impossible. What does one do, for example, when a telephonist in Indonesia tells you there is a three-week delay on a call to a remoter part of the country? What happens when one has (as we did once) a six-day flight delay in Nepal? What must it be like to live in a country where the telephones can be out of order for six months, and postal delays can take several weeks? Yet this is what life is like for most people in the world today.

We can also be frustrated in the West. Life can be unbearable for us too without the fruit of patience. Someone has called the newly constructed M25 motorway "the largest car park in Britain". What do we do when caught in lengthy traffic jams? Every day presents us with trials which test our patience. And this is even more true when we extend this into the area of the Church. How frustrated we can be with people. How slowly renewal grows. How long we have to wait for people to accept the gifts of the Spirit and move in their power. Patience, patience, patience!

A key verse for me in the epistle to the Hebrews is 6:12, "We do not want you to become lazy, but to imitate those who through faith and patience inherit what has been promised." In this letter the writer refers a number of times to Abraham, the model man of faith in the Old Testament. How patient he was! God told him he was going to have a son, but he had to wait many years before it came true. All through this time his wife Sarah was not getting any younger. We need both faith and patience.

Patience is so important when we are ministering the gifts of the Spirit. We are so often in a hurry, especially when we are praying for sick people. We pray once and press on. We need to wait to see the work of the Spirit in people. Things don't happen all at once. The Pentecostals sometimes made too much of "tarrying" as they called it for the Lord to bless them. We seem to have gone to the other extreme. It is now instant blessing or no blessing at all. But a "take it or leave it" attitude is foreign to God. He is infinitely patient with us, as we should be with one another.

Kindness

Here the Greek word used is *chrestotes*. We notice at once that the word is similar to "Christ". It was a favourite name in Roman times for a slave. We presume that "kindness" was a quality expected of them. At all events the two words *chrestos* and *christos* may have been confused, and in Antioch, where they were first called "Christians", the believers may have been called "the goody-goodies".

At all events, the word describes generosity, or a generous spirit. Jesus described His yoke as "easy" (Matthew 11:30), and the same word is used. He meant that it does not chafe, it is kind to one's neck! Perhaps "kind" would be a better word, for "easy" is hardly the right word to describe the Christian life. The way we relate to one another should be like this too. We should not chafe one another.

It is also a word used to define "love" in 1 Corinthians 13:4. "Love", Paul writes, "is patient, love is kind". A generous spirit is part of what true love is. One can see how vital it is to mix this fruit with the gifts of the Holy Spirit. The Lord has a generous spirit. He is reckless in what He gives and to whom He gives it. We need this kind of spirit when we are sharing the spiritual gifts with others. A Scrooge-like spirit is unhelpful.

Goodness

There is a sharper note to this word than the previous one. "Kindness" helps, but "goodness" can rebuke and chastise. When Jesus cleared the temple He displayed goodness (Mark 11:15–17); when He responded to the sinful woman who anointed His feet, He showed kindness (Luke 7:36–50).

There is a need for both. Charles Erdmans defines this word as "love in action". This is surely what the gifts of the Spirit are. Goodness is an energetic principle. It is what we do in response to human situations when a need is found.

The short form of this word is used to describe Barnabas. In Acts 11:24, it was said of him that he was "a good man" as well as full of the Holy Spirit. The way he looked after Paul, and later Mark, are object lessons for us all. We have shown in Chapter 5 that a key to spiritual maturity is discovering one's gifts, and encouraging the gifts that others have. Barnabas was the first to see the potential in Paul. Later he was to disagree with Paul about Mark, and to help him to find his gifts and use them. Goodness will always do this. Imagine the New Testament without the writings of Mark and Paul! What a debt we owe to Barnabas for his talent spotting which was the fruit of goodness in his life.

Faith

We have already looked at "faith" as it applies to the gifts of the Spirit. Here we see it listed as a fruit. When we see the importance the New Testament attaches to faith we are not surprised to see it here. This fruit plays a vital role in the creating of true fellowship, and as a moral quality it is one of the most crucial. Faith will include loyalty, dependability, and trust.

When the gifts of the Spirit begin to appear in the life and worship of our church, trust is often at risk. It is easy to be suspicious and critical. The threat of division can add pressure to act disloyally. We need to be open with one another, and share whenever appropriate, so that facts are not hidden and so become twisted or distorted. We must trust each other.

Gentleness

The Greek word is translated in some versions "humility" or "meekness", as well as "gentleness". Meekness is sometimes confused with "weakness". That is a mistake. The word implies "power under control" and is, therefore, a most suitable quality when it comes to handling the gifts of the Spirit.

Jesus once described Himself as "gentle" (Matthew 11:29). It is not a word one normally links with greatness. It was Napoleon who claimed that God was always "on the side of the big battalions". But Jesus claimed the opposite. In the Sermon on the Mount He said it was the meek who would inherit the earth (Matthew 5:5). Someone has said "the rock that resists the crowbar, gives way to the roots of the tender plant". The macadamised driveway will support a car weighing several tons, but is broken through by a daffodil weighing a few ounces! The quality of gentleness has that kind of power about it. It does not bludgeon its way through, but by constant and gentle pressure can break through the stoniest of hearts.

True gentleness stems from faith in God and in oneself. Insecure people can be rude and strong-minded. They feel they have to wreak revenge on society and to retaliate for all the injustices they and others have had to endure. The person whose faith is strong does not need to resort to this.

The gifts of the Holy Spirit need to be handled gently. They are like a delicate piece of Dresden china. It is not fitting to throw them at people, or to deal crudely with those for whom they are intended. Much harm has been done by rough methods. The fruit of gentleness will help us handle them properly.

Self-control

We have come full circle, and this final fruit leads us back again to the first one. True love will always be expressed within the context of self-control. The more powerfully we love, the more

Gifted People

we will be in control of ourselves. To give way to lust is the opposite of love, for lust is lack of self-control.

The word self-control suggests this is something that we do. We control ourselves. But we all know that we cannot do that. Left to ourselves we do and say the most terrible things. Without the restraining work of the Spirit in our lives we are prone to many evils.

No, self-control is not a stoical gritting of the teeth. For here it is included in a list of the fruit of the Spirit. It is something that is grown in us by God, not something we try to grow ourselves. While the Spirit requires our willing co-operation, it is He not us who does the controlling.

Sometimes people think of self-control as emotional restraint. No, we have far too much of that in our Anglo-Saxon heritage! To be able to weep and laugh, shout for joy, and raise the rafters with our singing is to allow the Spirit to control us rather than our cultural roots. God has given us emotions, and we are not to lock them up in a box. We must allow the Spirit to use them and let them be expressed.

The gifts of the Spirit need the fruit of self-control if they are to build up the Church. Compulsiveness suggests being out of control. Compulsive Charismatics are a problem. It is no good saying, when we act unlovingly, "I had to." The Spirit of God is the Spirit of self-control. He restrains as well as constrains us. He sees to it that what we do and say is controlled by Him not by ourselves or by others.

*   *   *

Paul concludes the list of the fruit with the words, "Against such things there is no law" (Galatians 5:23). Paul is not saying that we are free now to ignore the law. He is saying the opposite. We are set free by the Spirit in order to keep the law. The action of the Spirit is to fulfil the law. There is no need for law when the law is being kept. To live as a Christian is to live in the Spirit, not live according to a code of morals. When the Spirit is in control the law is kept and not broken. He liberates us from legalism and the fruit of the Spirit is the evidence that this has happened.

Legalism has robbed many believers of their birthrights. This is nowhere more clear than in the area covered by this book. Legalism inhibits charismatic experiences. One of the best stories Jesus ever told was about the Prodigal Son (Luke 15:11–32). The angry elder brother is so true to life. He complained to his father, " 'All these years I have been slaving for you and never disobeyed your orders. Yet you never gave me even a young goat so I could celebrate with my friends' " (v. 29). Many a person has felt like that, cheated by God. He has not given them what they really needed and desired. But they are as wrong about this as the elder brother was.

The father's gentle answer is a classic. " 'My son, you are always with me, and everything I have is yours' " (v. 31). There is no place for greed or envy in the Kingdom of God. The wonderful gifts of the Spirit are available from the hands of the Father for everyone. His gifts are our gifts to share with others. We don't need to live in spiritual poverty, when He has so much to give us. We are all prodigals in one way or another. But there is no need for us to be elder brothers as well.

REFERENCES

1 *The 20th Century Pentecostal/Charismatic Renewal in the Holy Spirit, with its goal of world evangelization*, David Barrett, published by the International Bulletin of Missionary Research, 1988.

2 *Welcome, Holy Spirit, a Study of Charismatic Renewal in the Church*, Larry Christenson, Augsburg Publishing House, 1987, p. 85–86.

3 *ibid.*, p. 175.

4 *Nine O'Clock in the Morning*, Dennis Bennett, Kingsway, 1974.

5 *Gifts of the Holy Spirit*, Cecil Cousen, Kingsway, 1986.

6 *Money, Sex and Power*, Richard Foster, Hodder & Stoughton, 1985, p. 175.

PERSONAL PROFILES

Barrett, David
Anglican missiologist and author of *World Christian Encyclopedia.*

Bennett, Dennis
Episcopal priest, former Rector of St. Luke's Episcopal Church, Seattle, USA, and author of the best seller *Nine O'Clock in the Morning.*

Bittlinger, Arnold
German scholar and European charismatic leader.

Bonhoeffer, Dietrich
A leader of the German "Confessing Church" in the Thirties, which opposed the rise of Nazism. Executed by the Gestapo in the closing stages of World War 2.

Bonkke, Reinhard
German evangelist educated in Wales who has worked extensively in Africa with some of the largest meetings in evangelistic history (one in Nigeria drawing over 250,000 people).

Christenson, Larry
One of the best known leaders in the Charismatic Renewal. An American Lutheran he has ministered all over the world

and written many books including the best seller *The Christian Family*. One of the founder members of the Singapore Consultation (now called the International Charismatic Consultation on World Evangelisation or ICCOWE).

Cousen, Cecil
A Yorkshireman, member of the Pentecostal Apostolic Church and a leader in the "Latter Rain" revival in Canada in the Fifties. One of the first Pentecostals to pray openly for people to receive the baptism in the Spirit rather than the tradition of "tarrying". Died in 1989.

Double, Don
Founder of the *Good News Crusade*, which is based in Cornwall, England. International evangelist.

Du Plessis, David
South African born Pentecostal leader who can be called the father of the modern Charismatic Renewal. Affectionately called "Mr. Pentecost", he was a man of love, faith and truth. He died in 1987.

England, Edward
For many years Religious Editor and Director of the publishers Hodder & Stoughton. Now Director of Highland Books, literary agent for over 100 authors, and editor of *Renewal* magazine.

Forrest, Tom
Catholic priest and Director of *Evangelisation 2000*. One of the founder members of the Singapore Consultation (see also *Christenson, Larry*).

Greenwood, Harry
British Pentecostal evangelist who pioneered a strong "signs and wonders" ministry. Died in 1988.

Kuhlman, Kathryn

The world's most widely known woman evangelist. Once a month for over 10 years she filled the 7,000 seats of the Shrine Auditorium in Los Angeles. Died in 1976.

Roberts, Oral

America's premier healing evangelist, and the most famous Pentecostal in the world. Founder of the University named after him in Tulsa, Oklahoma.

Sanford, Agnes

Pioneer of "inner healing" ministries. Wife of an Episcopal priest she was the first to teach about the "healing of the memories". She died in 1982.

Wigglesworth, Smith

One of the early leaders of the Pentecostal Movement in Great Britain. Known as "the Bradford plumber", he held healing meetings all over the world. The first to recognise the strategic future ministry of David du Plessis.

Wimber, John

Founding pastor of the Vineyard Christian Fellowship in Anaheim, California. Leading pioneer of "power evangelism", evangelism done with signs and wonders.

Other Books of Interest by Servant Publications

Christianity with Power
Discovering the Truth about Signs and Wonders
Charles H. Kraft

Power. Politicians crave it. Money buys it. And some people will do anything for it. In a world where New Agers rely on crystals and channeling to tap into spiritual power, the Christian is reminded that Jesus used supernatural power to heal the sick, cast out demons, and raise the dead.

Yet many modern Christians have become embarassed and reluctant to preach a gospel accompanied by supernatural power. Is it because our western worldview conditions us to fit God into a neat, predictable mold? How can we escape worldview captivity? Step by step, Charles Kraft shows the limits of our western worldview and offers us biblical understanding of signs and wonders. Learn how your worldview affects your experience of spiritual power and what you can do about it. *$8.95*

Signs, Wonders, and the Kingdom of God
A Biblical Guide for the Reluctant Skeptic
Don Williams

This new book on signs and wonders presents a fascinating, biblical theology of the kingdom of God. Dr. Williams describes how God works to establish his reign now and in eternity and how we can demonstrate and proclaim, as Jesus did, the supernatural power of his kingdom.

Signs, Wonders, and the Kingdom of God investigates the relationship between supernatural power and the ministry of the church today. As a community of love and faith under the reign of God, we can continue Jesus' ministry of power: evangelizing the poor, casting out demons, healing the sick, and setting free the captives. A compelling look at the kingdom of God from the perspective of signs and wonders. *$7.95*